THE POSTHUMOUS ESSAYS
OF JOHN CHURTON COLLINS

J. Churton Collins

From the oil painting by George Phoenix.
of Wolverhampton.

THE
POSTHUMOUS ESSAYS OF
JOHN CHURTON COLLINS
EDITED BY L. C. COLLINS

LONDON : J. M. DENT & SONS LTD.
NEW YORK : E. P. DUTTON & CO.
1912

34434

PREFACE

MOST of the following Essays were delivered by my father in the form of lectures. My task has been to put into shape passages which were little more than rough notes, to find references for the quotations given, and generally to see the Essays through the press.

Amongst those who knew him some speculation may be aroused as to whether or not the quotations which are given throughout the book were written down by him from memory. Certainty on this point is impossible, but the nature of the few slips which occurred in the quoted extracts has induced me to think that the majority at least of the quotations were written down without reference to their originals; and to those who were acquainted with his wonderful memory, and to the readers of his " Life," recently published, this would be no matter for surprise. As regards quoted extracts, which are still copyright, I have sought and obtained permission for their retention where the debt is a big one, in other words, where

" matter " has been quoted somewhat freely ; where the debt is a slight one, I trust that the acknowledgment of its source will be considered as a sign of indebtedness, and that the omission of a formal request for the inclusion of such a quotation will not be looked upon as due to a want of courtesy.

The essay on " Shakespearean Theatres," and that portion of the essay on Browning entitled " Browning and Butler," have been published since his death, and I desire to thank the editors of the *Contemporary Review* for their courtesy in allowing me to republish them here.

The article on " Popular Proverbs," which I have also included, is not posthumous, having appeared in 1902 in the *New Liberal Review*, a magazine which eight years ago ceased publication.

In conclusion, I have to thank Mr. George Phoenix, of Wolverhampton, for allowing me to reproduce the hitherto unpublished portrait as a frontispiece.

L. C. C.

April 1912

CONTENTS

SHAKESPEAREAN THEATRES

IT is not possible to determine the year in which Shakespeare arrived in London, but it seems pretty certain that it must have been some time between 1585 and 1588. Probability points to 1587, for in that year the two leading companies of players, the Queen's and Lord Leicester's, as well as two subordinate companies who were under the patronage of the Lords Essex and Stafford, visited Stratford-on-Avon, and it has been conjectured, with much plausibleness, that the young Shakespeare got connected with one of these companies in some capacity or other, or at least made friends in one of them, and so was induced to leave Stratford for London. In any case, we shall probably not be far wrong if we date his arrival in London in or about 1587.

I propose in this paper to deal, not with the literary influences nor with the social and political conditions which moulded this mighty genius and gave it the ply but with the physical mechanism, so to speak, through which it found expression—in other words, with our theatres, our stage and our actors, while Shakespeare was at work.

But a preliminary word or two will be necessary. From the middle of Henry VIII.'s reign there had been much dramatic activity, and every decade this had increased. The mysteries and miracles had been followed by the moralities and interludes, and these had been gradually developing into the regular drama. By 1572 the taste for dramatic entertainments had become a passion with the multitude, to the great scandal of sober and decorous citizens, and especially of the Puritans. Every impediment had been placed in the way of these amusements. It was only by placing themselves under the protection of some nobleman, who was responsible for their good behaviour, that players were allowed to exercise their profession. They existed purely on sufferance. As a rule they were not admitted within the boundaries of any town. Constantly threatened, in 1575 they were formally expelled from the City of London by the Mayor and Corporation. Regular playhouses there were none. Where performances were given they were given generally in inn-yards, the audiences being partly round the actors in the courtyard and partly in the gallery running round. In London favourite places were " The Belle Savage " on Ludgate Hill, " The Bell " and " The Cross Keys " in Gracechurch Street, and " The Bull " in Bishopsgate Street, but no doubt most of the larger inn-yards witnessed these entertainments. It was the year succeeding the expulsion of the players from the City which marks the most important epoch in the history of our stage, for in 1576 James Burbage erected our first theatre.

I must ask the reader to come a little journey

with me in imagination. Let us stand as nearly as we can on the sites of the theatres with which Shakespeare was either professionally connected or with which, at any rate, he was familiar. First, we take a ticket by the Underground Railway for Bishopsgate Street, make our way to the present Standard Theatre in Shoreditch High Street, walk past it a few paces, and take the first turning to the left. This brings us into Holywell Lane. Before us is the North London Railway arch; we pass through it, taking the first turn to the right, and we are on the site of the old Holywell Priory. We go on a few yards; to our left is King John's Court; to our right the North London viaduct; in front and running parallel with King John's Court is New Inn Yard. Either on the ground now covered by the stack of buildings intervening between King John's Court and New Inn Yard, or on the ground to our right intersected by the viaduct stood James Burbage's epoch-making structure. A simple circular enclosure, modelled no doubt on the two amphitheatres for bull and bear baiting on The Bankside, it was built of wood, and had, like the amphitheatre, no roof, but was open to the sky. Of its size we have no account, but as it was built simply of wood and yet cost Burbage between £600 and £700, and is described also as being "a gorgeous playing-house," it was probably of considerable dimensions.

Within a stone's-throw of "The Theatre" stood our second playhouse. We proceed leftward down New Inn Yard, and we find ourselves

in the main thoroughfare, Curtain Road. The
second turning to the left is Hewett Street, late
Gloucester Street. This was formerly Curtain
Court. Here somewhere in the block of buildings,
possibly on the site of a carpenter's and furniture
shop (formerly the Great Eastern Saw Mills), or
beyond on what is now a timber yard, stood
" The Curtain." In structure it resembled " The
Theatre," and appears to have been erected about
the same time. These were the theatres with
which Shakespeare was in all likelihood first connected. " Henry V." was certainly performed at
" The Curtain," and almost certainly " Romeo
and Juliet," too. Tradition points to " The
Theatre " and " The Curtain " as the places where
he once held horses for the gallants who came to
the play. Before continuing our journey we must
not forget to glance at that fine and interesting
church, St. Leonard's, Shoreditch, which con-
tains the dust of so many of the fathers of our
stage, among them James Burbage, Richard
Burbage, Richard Cowley, William Sly, and that
Yorick of our early drama, Richard Tarleton.
Now we return to Bishopsgate Street and make
our way to Whitecross Street. We go straight
up, and we see on our left Play House Yard,
leading to Golden Lane. Just here is an enormous
stack of new buildings stretching between Play
House Yard and Roscoe Street ; on the site of
these buildings, with part of it abutting on
Golden Lane, stood the most magnificent of the
Elizabethan theatres, " The Fortune," and a
fortune indeed it was to Edward Alleyn. Its

exact position was between Rose Alley and Black
Swan Court. Black Swan Court has disappeared,
but Rose Alley still exists as an alley, though it
has now no name. "The Fortune" was erected
about 1598, and the indenture between Henslowe
and Edward Alleyn on the one side and Peter
Street on the other is still extant, and gives us an
elaborate account of the structure. It was to be
constructed eighty feet square on the outside
and fifty-five feet square within; the boxes,
rooms, and galleries were to be three stories high.
The total cost of the site and the building was
£1320. Turn now into Golden Lane through
Play House Yard, bear to the left along Old
Street and Clerkenwell Road, then bend to the
right along St. John Street, Clerkenwell, till you
come to Aylesbury Street; go down it for a few
yards, and you will see on your right hand
Woodbridge Street. This was formerly Red
Bull Yard, and here stood "The Red Bull"
Theatre, on the site most probably of what is now
Hayward's Place; and, continuing, keep along
to the left through Aylesbury Street to Farringdon
Market and down the old course of the Fleet
River till you come to Blackfriars, and there
within the ancient Dominican precincts, near
the Pipe Office and next to the house of Sir
George Cary (an area now covered by modern
business premises), Burbage built The Black
Friars Theatre in 1596. Near at hand the old
hall of the White Friars Monastery was used for
acting from 1610, and near this spot the White
Friars playhouse was built in 1629. Farther west,

in Drury Lane, was " The Cockpit," later known
as " The Phœnix."   But it is now time to cross
the Thames to the grimy, malodorous Borough
Market, lying under the south side of Cannon
Street bridge, and you are on the classic ground
of The Bankside. A few paces bring you to
Barclay and Perkins' Brewery. Somewhere on
the area covered by that brewery stood " The
Globe " Theatre, built in 1599 by Cuthbert and
Richard Burbage out of the materials of The
Theatre in Shoreditch, which was demolished
during the preceding year. This is the theatre
particularly associated with Shakespeare, where
most of his plays between 1599 and 1613 were
performed, and of which he was part proprietor.
It was one of the most purely popular theatres.
Like those of " The Fortune," the actors were
terrible leer-throats, says Gayton.*   Go on a few

* This footnote and the one following were added in the
Contemporary Review, January 1911, when the article was
originally published :

Reference may be made to the discussion over the actual
date of The Globe Theatre which occurred in the Press at the
end of 1909, based upon documentary evidence brought forward
by Dr. Wallace, of Nebraska, U.S.A.   Dr. Wallace affirmed that
he had proof of the site of The Globe Playhouse being on the
north side of Park Street, opposite to the spot hitherto accepted
as correct. The situation had a pungent interest, as exactly one
week after Dr. Wallace's discoveries were published in *The Times*
Sir Herbert Beerbohm Tree was due to unveil a mural tablet
erected by " The Shakespeare Reading Society " on a wall of
Messrs. Barclay and Perkins' Brewery, standing on the south side
of Park Street. However, further documents were discovered ;
for instance, one in the Record Office, dated 1625, and one in the

paces and you will see Rose Alley. Here stood " The Rose," the proprietor of which was the astute Henslowe, and which was probably erected about 1587. Close by this was The Bear Garden, still so called,* and this is the site of the famous Bear Garden, or Bear House, a building serving the double purpose of bear-baiting and of dramatic entertainments. It was the first theatre instituted on The Bankside, though when plays began there we do not know. In 1613, after the destruction of The Globe Theatre by fire, this Bear Garden was transformed into " The Hope," and became a very flourishing

possession of the solicitors of Messrs. Barclay and Perkins, dated 1715, which led to an almost complete chain of evidence identifying the correct site of The Globe Playhouse as being where tradition has placed it.

The Commemorative Tablet, stating, " Here stood The Globe Playhouse of Shakespeare, 1598–1613," was duly fixed on the traditional site and unveiled on October 8, 1909. Dr. Wallace discovered, *vide The Times* of October 2 and 4, 1909, that Shakespeare owned twice as many shares in The Black Friars as in The Globe Theatre, but that the latter theatre was twice as profitable.

Shakespeare's annual share of The Globe never exceeded £300, and possibly not so much. It appears, therefore, that his income from the two theatres did not exceed £600. This, it must be remembered, meant much more 300 years ago than it does to-day. Mr. Harold Child, in vol. vi. of the " Cambridge History of English Literature " (pp. 241–279), discussed " The Elizabethan Theatre " at length.—[ED. *C.R.*]

* It is in fact called " Bear Gardens." In the lane is an ancient disused building which is locally regarded as the old theatre. Close at hand is " The White Bear " public-house.— [ED. *C.R.*]

theatre till nearly the end of the seventeenth century. Some years ago the skulls and bones of bears were often found about here, and there is now a public-house in The Bear Garden where these relics may be seen. Close by The Bear Garden Shakespeare lodged, and if he did not often drop into " The Falcon," all we can say is that he was not the man we take him to have been, or he must have preferred " The Dancing Bear." Making our way onwards towards Black-friars Bridge, we find ourselves on or close to what must have been the site of " The Swan." It must have stood on the space now covered by the street a few feet south of Southwark Street and Stamford Street, near the Blackfriars Railway Goods Station. It was erected as a speculation by a London citizen, one Francis Langley, and was completed in 1598, and was one of the finest of the London theatres. A most interesting drawing of the interior of this theatre has within the last few years been discovered in the University Library of Utrecht, and has been reproduced and published in a most interesting pamphlet by Dr. Gaedertz. But as it is not an original drawing made in the theatre, but is drawn from some description given in a letter or by word of mouth, we must not attach too much importance to it. One other theatre and its site remain to complete this topographical sketch. It would seem, from Henslowe's diary, that in 1594 Newington Butts was a flourishing centre of dramatic activity, plays by Marlowe, Greene, Shakespeare and others having been acted in that suburb; but there is no proof that there was any theatre erected there, the evidence for the existence of such a structure in Shakespeare's time being purely inferential. But Professor Hales tells me on the authority of a distinguished antiquary, whose name he is not at liberty to mention, that there *was* a theatre there, and that its site was marked by a place called Play House Yard, since known under different names—Back Alley, Bloomsbury Square, Anne's Place—and that it lay, in fact, between the present Clock Passage, Newington Butts, Swan Place and Hampton Street.

Such, then, were the sites of the principal theatres in Shakespeare's time. At the beginning of his career he was associated probably with The Theatre, certainly with The Curtain, The Rose, and The Newington Butts, and after 1596 with The Black Friars and The Globe. The company to which he belonged was the Lord Chamberlain's, afterwards, on the accession of James I., known as the King's, and under the auspices of this company all his plays, with two exceptions—namely, "Titus Andronicus" and "The Third Part of Henry VI."—were produced.

It is difficult for us in these days to realise the conditions under which Shakespeare's plays were first presented. Let us consider them. First, let us take the structure of a typical Elizabethan theatre. It was built of wood, its form being circular or hexagonal, being modelled in its general structure on the old amphitheatres for bull and bear baiting; in its internal structure on the old inn-yards; and, if we take the large ones like The Fortune, Globe, and Swan, was capable of holding from three to five hundred people. I strike an average from various accounts. The building was roofless, open to the sky, so that those who occupied the upper galleries and the ground, as it was called, or pit, could be scorched by the sun or drenched by the rain; but the actors were protected from the weather by a thatched penthouse, or roof, which projected over the back part of the stage. The stage, the width of which was some forty-three feet, projected into the pit or yard some twenty-three feet, leaving a space to left and right; it was raised above the level of the ground, and was, in the case of The Globe at least, protected by railings to prevent invasion by the groundlings. At the back of the stage, which was strewed with rushes, were the "tiring" rooms, where the actors dressed and from which they emerged from the arras or hangings on to the stage. Here, too, was a balcony or upper stage, which served for a mountain, the walls of a town, a tower, a window, or, indeed, any elevation which might be needed in the action of the play, as, for example, in " King John," "Henry VI.," "The Merchant of Venice," "Romeo and Juliet"; and from this, as from a pulpit, the prologuer sometimes spoke, and important speeches were delivered. Here, too, when a play within a play was represented, as in " The Taming of the Shrew" and " Hamlet," the actors in the inner play performed their part; in that case Hamlet and the King and Queen, with their attendants, would have their backs to the general audience.   Curtains, technically called traverses, were employed to divide the stage into rooms or tents, or to afford means of concealment. The roof of the stage, which was called the heavens, was apparently either painted a sky-blue or sky-blue drapery was suspended across it ; but if a tragedy was acted it was hung with black, and it was to this that Rosse pointed when he said :

> Thou seest the Heavens as troubled with man's act
> Threaten his bloody stage.

The curtain which concealed all this from the audience till the play began was not, as in our theatres, drawn up from above, but ran on rods, and was drawn from the middle right and left.* In some theatres it was woollen, in some it was made of silk.   There was no scenery in our sense of the term at all, only painted cloth or tapestry at the back.   The place where the action was supposed to be was indicated by a placard— London, The Rialto, Verona, Milford Haven, The Fields, A Wood, At Sea, &c.—or it was announced by the prologue or by one of the actors.   If a tavern was the scene, a table with pots and glasses was pushed forward ; if a bedroom, a bed.   The scenery was supplied by appeals to the imagination of the audience, such as Shakespeare makes in the prologue to "Henry V." :

> Piece out our imperfections with your thoughts :
> Into a thousand parts divide one man,
> And make imaginary puissance.

---

* In several of the London theatres now the curtain is drawn right and left from the centre.

> Think, when we talk of horses, that you see them
> Printing their proud hoofs i' the receiving earth,
> For 'tis your thoughts that now must deck our kings.

To this defect in scenery Sir Philip Sidney very pleasantly refers :

Now you shall have three ladies walk to gather flowers, and then we must believe the stage to be a garden. By-and-by we hear news of shipwreck in the same place, then we are to blame if we accept it not for a rock. Upon the back of that comes out a hideous monster with fire and smoke, and then the miserable beholders are bound to take it for a cave ; while in the meantime two armies fly in, represented with four swords and bucklers, and then what hard heart will not receive it for a pitched field ? *

Sidney was, of course, referring to the stage some twelve years before Shakespeare became connected with it, but his description exactly applies to the later Elizabethan theatre. In fact, the highly ornate and poetical cast of Shakespeare's diction is intended, by substituting an appeal to the imagination for an appeal to the eye, to supply the place of scenery. And in forgetting or ignoring this lies the great mistake which the modern stage makes in representing his plays. To trick them out in scenic pomp and magnificence and to lay excessive stress on externals is simply

> To gild refined gold, to paint the lily,
> To throw a perfume on the violet.†

A change of scene was simply effected by drawing the curtain up and down, or sometimes by the actors taking a few paces. There is a curious illustration of this in Greene's " Pinner of Wakefield,"

* " An Apologie for Poetry."   † " King John," iv. 2.

where one of the characters challenges another to
a fight at the town's end, they being then in the
middle of the town : " Come, sir, will you come
to the town's end now ?   Aye, sir.   Come then."
In the next line the speaker adds : " Now we are
at the town's end."

But what they wanted in scenery they made up
in noise and bustle—the discharge of small cannon,
flourishes of trumpets, beating of drums, the clash
of swords, rapiers, and cutlasses, loud shouts,
ringing of bells and the like kept things very
lively.   The only machinery employed consisted
of the balcony and traverses referred to, of trap-
doors, and of some sort of pulleys for managing
the descents of deities, angels, and saints.   So, in
Greene's " Alphonsus," " Let Venus be let down
from the top of the stage " ; and in another play,
" Fortune descends down from Heaven."   But
this machinery could not, it seems, be depended
upon for getting them up again.   So Greene
about his Venus : " Exit Venus, or if you can
conveniently let a chair come down from the
top of the stage and draw her up."   As on the
Greek stage, the dresses were sometimes very
gorgeous and expensive.   Thus among Henslowe's
items we find " a dress gowne of cloth of gold,"
" a damask cassock guarded with velvet," " white
satin layde thick with gold lace," " a payer of
rowne pandes hosse of cloth of silver, the panes
layd with gold lace."   And among his items is a
very curious one, for which even Mr. Maskelyne
would no doubt like to have the receipt, " a robe
for to go invisibell."

But to return to the structure of the theatre. There were two doors—one for the actors leading to the " tiring " rooms, the other for the public leading into the ground or yard. This, as I said before, answered to our pit, and in the private theatres, such as The Black Friars, was actually called the pit ; but in the public theatres either the yard or ground. This, with the upper gallery, was the cheapest part of the theatre, and a penny or twopence admitted you to this. There were no seats unless you chose to hire a stool, and the spectators either stood, sat, or sprawled on the floor, which was, when clean, strewn with rushes, but very shortly after the arrival of the audience it must have been as filthy and unsavoury as a pig-sty. On the horrors of that floor I shall not dilate. If you did not wish to sit down in a mash of broken meat and bread, of half-picked bones and half-munched apples, nut-husks and tobacco ashes, you could hire for sixpence a stool. But on the whole you would do well to make your way into the galleries, where you could get a seat at the same price, if you did not mind the reek steaming up from the " ground " and groundlings. These galleries, or stories, stretched in a semicircle behind and on each side of the stage, and were about twelve feet and a half in breadth, the lower about twelve feet in height the second about eleven, and the third about nine. The price of admission to the highest of these galleries was twopence, and it was called the twopenny gallery, but you might get in sometimes for a penny. Admission to the other galleries was sixpence. To the left and right of the stage under the galleries were the " rooms," answering to our boxes, and admission to these was, in Shakespeare's time, one shilling. To the balcony or upper stage were attached also two " rooms " which were called private, where visitors of distinction, who did not wish to be seen, could be accommodated; but being, as Dekker says, almost smothered in darkness, they were not generally sought, and could be got cheap. But if, being a man of mode, you wished to pose and be conspicuous, the thing to do was to get a seat on the stage, where you could, if you were minded, gracefully sprawl, or, what would be more comfortable, hire a three-legged stool to sit upon. This would only cost you a shilling, and the shilling would include the right of your page to come and light your pipe for you.

Now let us suppose that we are going to make an afternoon of it at the theatre when Shakespeare was in his glory at The Globe. It is about a quarter to three in the afternoon. We are on one of the stairs opposite St. Paul's, hailing a waterman. There over on the Surrey side the flags are already waving from the little wooden turrets of The Globe, The Rose, and The Swan, towering over and in gay contrast with the green trees behind and around. We embark. The river is alive with boats and wherries making their way to the stairs on The Bankside, and the scullers are doing a roaring trade, especially our old friend John Taylor, whose boat is half sunk with its freight of passengers ; knavishly loaden, as one wherryman has just observed with more than a twinge of jealousy. After being very nearly run down by a sailing vessel and very nearly colliding with two returning boats—the oaths and ribaldry interchanged at these junctures have been something frightful—we disembark at The Bear Garden stairs just opposite the right of The Globe. This " glory of the Bank and fort of the parish," as Ben Jonson calls it, is not an imposing building, with its shabby thatch fringe on the roof and the small apertures which pierce and dot its dingy wooden sides.

Of the entertainment which is awaiting us we can be in no doubt, for there it is in staring red letters on several placards, two of which are plastered on the theatre and one on a tree and one on a wall; it is also being bawled out by vociferous " posts," presumably for the benefit of those who cannot read :

A most pleasant, excellent and conceited comedie of Syr John Falstaffe and the " Merrie Wives of Windsor," entermixed with sundrie variable and pleasing humours of Sir Hugh the Welsh Knight, Justice Shallow and his wise cousin, Mr. Slender. With the swaggering vaine of Ancient Pistol and Corporal Nym. As it hath been divers times acted by the Right Honorable my Lord Chamberlaine's Servants, both before her Majesty and elsewhere.

We must make haste, for it has gone three, and the trumpet has sounded twice, and in a minute or two the third blast will blare out and the curtain will be drawn. There are two doors— one leading into the yard and one to the " tiring " house and the stage. We take the latter, that

we may get a stool on the stage.   This we arrange
without difficulty, seat ourselves comfortably, and
look about us.   The first thing that strikes us on
surveying the audience is that there is no lady to
be seen, no woman with any pretension to
refinement, unless the two sitting in the rooms
with masks on be such.   Some of the prentices
have brought their sweethearts, and a few, plainly
belonging to the humbler citizens, their wives.
Flaunting and impudent harridans there are in
abundance ; in fact, our neighbour on the stage,
who has just crept from behind the arras with his
three-footed stool in one hand and with the
sixpence to pay for it daintily mounted between
his forefinger and thumb in the other, has already
begun to bandy questionable compliments with
one of them in the first gallery.   A glance round
will show that a more motley and mixed assembly
could hardly have come together.   In the upper
gallery and in the yard the majority consists of
the very scum and rinsings of humanity, ignorant,
brutal, and filthy ; and side by side with them
a few—not many—respectable and quiet-looking
citizens ; but the most numerous class are
roystering prentices.   On the stage and in the
rooms are fashionable dandies, swashbucklers and
young bloods, as they were called, writers for the
theatres and actors ; these had always a free pass.
The theatre is full.   The occupations of those
assembled are as various as their callings and
characters.   Some are noisily playing cards or
dice ; some are smoking women as well as men ;
others are munching apples, discussing a herring-

B

pie, uncorking beer-bottles, or cracking nuts.
Some are reading books, some are preparing their
tables to take notes of the play that they may get
by heart the passages which please them or retail
in ridicule among the taverns those that do not.
Among these is one man on whom the actors will
keep an eye ; he is a noted literary pirate who,
if he can, will take down the play, or as much as
he can manage, in shorthand, and so cheat the
company out of the copyright.   In one corner of
the yard two men are fighting, the bystanders
cheering them on ; in another there is a very lively
altercation between a defrauded waterman and
his escaped freight.   The third trumpet sounds ;
there is a sudden hush in this Babel ; the curtain
is drawn, and the play begins.   An actor in a long
black velvet cloak threads his way among those
who are sprawling or sitting on the stage and
delivers the prologue.   While the play is being
acted the audience are tolerably quiet.   But the
din between the acts is deafening, for while
trumpets, recorders, hautboys, lutes, and fiddles,
most or some, are in full blast, the people in the
yard are bawling up to those in the galleries and
those in the galleries are bawling down to those in
the yard.   There is no reticence, no restraint.   The
play is freely and loudly criticised; so are the actors.
And approbation has not been universal, especially
among your neighbours on the stage.   Before the
second act was over one of them had risen up
from his tripod with a screwed and discontented
face and had tried to induce his acquaintances, by
becks and gestures, to annoy the actors by leaving

the theatre. To this they had not responded, and ever since he has been relieving his feelings by mewing at eloquent passages, shrugging his shoulders at hits and points, and whistling while the songs were being sung as loudly as he dare. There is now silence for the third act. But suddenly you become aware that there is universal commotion in the yard, which soon swells into uproar. A pickpocket has been caught red-handed. In an instant a dozen hands have seized him, and he is dragged along to the proscenium ; the performance stops ; he is hoisted over the rails on to the stage, the actors assisting in the operation, and bound with cords to one of the pillars which support the heavens. The play then goes on, and between the remaining acts the yard and galleries make it extremely lively for him. The play has lasted rather over two hours, and on the whole—for the din and smell are so oppressive—you are not sorry when the actors drop down on their knees to pray for the Queen and you can get away.

What I have given you has been the description of a comparatively quiet afternoon, when the audience were orderly and pleased. It was a very different scene when the majority of that audience were not pleased and the roughs got the bit between their teeth. If they did not like a play they kept up a running commentary of vitupera-tion and ridicule—mewing, yelling, hissing, bel-lowing, and even pelting the actors and driving them off the stage. They would force the actors to perform another play, and, if they did not accede to the request, tear down the benches and tiles, belabour and pelt the actors with them, and wreck the stage.   Shrove Tuesday was always a dreadful day.

But there was another class of theatres very different from these, called private theatres, such as one in White Friars, The Cockpit in Drury Lane, and the Singing School of St. Paul's ; but the most celebrated of these, and the one especially associated with Shakespeare, was The Black Friars. These were enclosed buildings.   What was called the " yard " was here called the " pit," and it was furnished with seats. The boxes, or rooms, were enclosed and furnished with locks, to which the hirers had keys. The performances were often at night, and were by candle-light, even when the plays were acted in the daytime.   The prices for admission were higher and the audiences much more select, ladies being present, and they were open in the winter, when the public theatres were always closed. The difference between the audiences at the public and private theatres, between those assembled at The Black Friars and those at The Globe, is well illustrated in the prologue to one of Shirley's plays, " The Doubtful Heir."   The play was performed at The Globe, but was written for Black Friars.   The prologue contemptuously addresses the audience thus :

> Gentlemen, I am only sent to say
> Our author did not calculate his play
> For *this* meridian.   The Bankside he knows
> Is far more skilful at the ebbs and flows
> Of water, than of wit.

It was for the audiences of the private theatres of The Black Friars that Shakespeare wrote. It is very probable that the grosser passages of low comedy which are so common in his plays were expressly interpolated for his Bankside audience at The Globe. He indemnified himself for this degradation, and so did Ben Jonson and others, by taking every opportunity of expressing his loathing and contempt for the rabble. But the question of public and private theatres is a very difficult one. It would seem that occasionally the public theatres were used as private. However, I must not go into this question; I have not space to discuss it. Performances were also given at the Inns of Court and at the Court. Neither Queen Elizabeth nor James I., nor any of the upper class, unless *incognito*, ever visited a public theatre. Plays were given at night so as not to interfere with the day performances of the actors.

And now a word or two about the actors. The Roscius or Garrick of the Shakespearean stage was James Burbage. He played all the great parts in Shakespeare, being, indeed, to Shakespeare what Tlepolemus was to Sophocles and Cephisophon to Euripides. Shylock, Richard III., Prince Henry, Romeo, Henry V., Brutus, Hamlet, Othello, Lear, Macbeth, Coriolanus—these were especially associated with him. How completely he was identified with Richard III. is very amusingly illustrated by Bishop Corbet, who tells us that his host at Leicester—

When he would have said King Richard died,
And called a horse! a horse! he Burbage cried.

Like Garrick and Robson, he was under the middle height and rather stout, and it was to adapt the part to him that Shakespeare makes the Queen say of Hamlet, "He's fat and scant of breath." Flecknoe, who must have known many who saw him act, says—

He was a delightful Proteus, so wholly transforming himself into his part and pulling off himself with his clothes as he never, not so much as in the "tiring" house, assumed himself again until the play was done. He had all the parts of an excellent orator, animating his words with speaking and speech with action.

Another writer speaks of his "wondrous tongue"; another says of him:

What a wide world was in that little space,
Thyself a world—The Globe thy fittest place,
Thy stature small, but every thought and mood
Might thereby from thy face be understood.

Next to Burbage in reputation was Edward Alleyne, the proprietor of The Fortune, and afterwards the founder of Dulwich College; but there is no evidence that he acted in Shakespeare's plays. Very celebrated also was Joseph Taylor, who played Hamlet, we are told, incomparably, and no wonder, if Downes is to be believed, for he was coached by no less a person than Shakespeare himself. Taylor was also great in Iago. Next comes John Lowin, whom Shakespeare specially instructed in the part of Henry VIII. He also acted Falstaff with "special applause." Among the best comic actors, who took the part of clowns, was ebullient Will Kemp, who danced the whole way—what merry days those must

have been !—from London to Norwich.   He was
the original Dogberry.   But Kemp had a bad
habit, and would insist on extemporising in his
part and carrying a clown's licence into regular
drama.   It is supposed that the provoked
Shakespeare was glancing at Kemp when he
wrote in " Hamlet " :

Let those that play your choruses speak no more than is set
down for them, for there be of them that will themselves laugh
to set on some quality of barren spectators to laugh too, though
in the meantime some necessary question of the play be then to
be considered : that's villainous and shows a most pitiful ambition
in the fool that uses it.

Other distinguished comic actors were Thomas
Pope, who was great on rustics and peasants ;
Richard Cowley, who played Verges ; Robert
Armin, who shone in fools and knaves ; and
Augustine Phillips.

I need hardly remind you that in Shakespeare's
time the parts of women were always taken by
boys or young men, which continued to be the
custom till Charles II.'s reign.   It is said that on
one occasion the King got very impatient at the
delay in the actors making their appearance, and
angrily demanded of the manager the reason.
" Beg your Majesty's pardon," said that func-
tionary, " but the queen is not shaved."   This
led, we are told, to the introduction of queens
who would not delay performances in the same
manner.   Among the most distinguished of those
who took female parts in Shakespeare's plays
were Alexander Cooke, Nicholas Tooley, and
William Ostler.   That Shakespeare must have

been a consummate master of the theory of acting is evident from the famous instructions in "Hamlet," but as an actor he does not seem to have been distinguished. We know that he acted in two several comedies or interludes before Queen Elizabeth at Greenwich, and also in Ben Jonson's "Every Man in His Humour" and "Sejanus," as well as in his own plays, and tradition asserts that he played the Ghost in "Hamlet" and Adam in "As You Like It."

The profession of playwright was not unlucrative. The highest price known to have been paid for a play was £10—that is, in our money, £100. Henslowe never paid more than £8. The ordinary price was £6—in our money, £60. Ben Jonson told Drummond in 1619 that he had only cleared £200—that is, in our money, about £2000—by all his plays written up to that time. With regard to the actors, it is very difficult to say what they made. They were distinguished into whole-sharers, three-quarter-sharers, and hired men. It is probable that the money taken at The Globe—which seems to have varied from £9 to £20—was divided into forty portions ; fifteen of these went to the proprietors, twenty-two to the actors, while three were retained for the purchase of new plays ; but the actor's income naturally fluctuated, depending as Collier says, upon the number of subdivisions, upon the popularity of his company, upon the stock plays belonging to it, the extent of its wardrobe, and the nature of its properties. The hired men or inferior actors received a regular stipend, which seems to have been from six to eight shillings a week. Perhaps if we put a leading actor's salary at about £400 a year we shall not be far wrong. Shakespeare and Alleyne made their fortunes not by acting, but by other business transactions, many of which had no connection with the stage. The social position of actors and playwrights in Shakespeare's time was anything but an enviable one, and Shakespeare has spoken with great bitterness of the sense of humiliation felt by him in reference to his profession.

SAMUEL JOHNSON

NOT very long ago I happened to be exploring an old bookshop and, turning over some pamphlets, I found, written on the title-page of one of them, the following epigram which, so far as I know, has not yet found its way into print:

> A parson of too free a life,
>   Was yet renown'd for noble preaching,
> And many grieved to see the strife
>   Between his practice and his teaching.
> At last his flock rebellious grew:
>   "My friends," he said, "the simple fact is
> Nor I nor you can both things do,
>   But I can preach and you can practise."

Now I don't know how it is, but I can't keep that anecdote from coming into my head when I read Carlyle's Lectures on Hero-Worship.

You will remember that in his Lecture on the hero as Man of Letters he does Dr. Johnson the honour to give him a place, and after a due amount of italicised Carlylese about " the infinites," " the enormous facts of the Universe glaring in for ever wonderful," and the like he proceeds to his sermon. Of that sermon I need say no more: we have all heard it, and have each been affected by it in our several ways. Most of us have probably quite as high an opinion of Dr. Johnson's greatness as Carlyle had, and as Carlyle, to say the least

of it, was a little too fond, was certainly unpleas-
antly fond, of harping on *our* littlenesses, our
meannesses, our unveracities that he might exalt
the stature of his hero by contrast, why should not
the worm turn—why should we not assume in self-
defence the same licence and render our tribute
to Johnson the more adequate by contrasting
him with his eulogist ?   Thanks to James Boswell,
thanks to James Anthony Froude, the two men
are laid bare to our inspection : we know them as
if we had lived with them—nay, infinitely better
—for then we should have seen through a glass
darkly—seen their mere doings, not understood
their motives ; heard their words, not read their
thoughts ; seen a part, not a whole—but now all is
clear.   I will not draw any contrasting parallel
between them, you can do that for yourselves—it
will not be difficult ; it will suggest itself *sotto
voce* as we proceed.

To no man of whom Biography holds record
was life a heavier burden than it was to Johnson.
He had inherited one of the most terrible of
physical maladies, and one of the most terrible
of mental maladies, a malady which in his own
words " made him mad all his life, or at least
not sober."   He told one of his friends that he
had never lived one week in his life that he
would live over again, were an angel to make the
proposal to him.   His whole life was an attempt
to escape from himself.   What pathos there is in
this one remark which he made to William Gerard
Hamilton, who had called on him and whom he
was accompanying to the door :

" I am very unwilling to be left alone, sir, and therefore I go with my company down the first pair of stairs, in some hopes that they may, perhaps, return again." *

His literary work was absolutely loathsome to him —he always worked against time and against the grain.   He cared little for fame, and very little for the applause of the world.   And yet, though life was so sore a burden to him, the fear of death was an agony.   On one occasion when Boswell had got him to talk on it—that thoughtless man, with characteristic want of tact, pressed the subject though Johnson plainly wished to avoid it—

He was [says Boswell] thrown into such a state of agitation that he expressed himself in a way that alarmed and distressed me ; showed an impatience that I should leave him, and when I was going away called to me sternly, "Don't let us meet to-morrow."*

Few men have been more sincerely and essentially religious than Johnson, and yet few men appear to have found less comfort from religion.   As Macaulay beautifully expresses it :

The light from heaven shone on him indeed, but not in a direct line, or with its own pure splendour. The rays had to struggle through a disturbing medium : they reached him refracted, dulled and discoloured by the thick gloom which had settled on his soul ; and though they might be sufficiently clear to guide him, were too dim to cheer him.†

Only think then of the heroism this man displayed in accomplishing what he did and in subduing himself to the conditions of his life in living up to his own words :

* Boswell's " Life of Johnson."
† " Essay on Samuel Johnson."

Every man must accept existence cheerfully under the
condition on which it has been granted to him.*

In conquering *himself* think of the Herculean task
of that Dictionary—of the stern, stubborn, conscientious labour involved in it, labour quadrupled
by the difficulties under which it was produced;
look at those voluminous writings filling twelve
volumes octavo in which you will not find one
careless or slovenly sentence. And notice how he
kept all his gloomy thoughts to himself—they
merely peeped out in the confidences of private
intimacy : no complaining, no tedious arraign-
ments of the scheme of things ["Sir," he once
said, "I hate a complainer"], no standing in
the middle of the road and cursing at large, but
wholesome, manly, cheerful talk with sound
advice and a "God speed you" for every one who
deserved it; very rough sometimes, irritable and
overbearing, not suffering fools gladly or at all
enduring shams, but, as Goldsmith said, with
"nothing of the bear but his skin" and never
bearing hardly on the weak and defenceless. With
most men the difficulties with which Johnson had
to struggle—disease, sorrow, poverty, Fortune's
injustices, the tardy recognition, the stinted wage
—are hardening influences. But the only effect
they had on that large and tender heart was to
make it larger and tenderer still. His generous
humanity to the distressed, says Boswell, was
almost beyond belief. A large part of his income
he gave away in charity. His very house he

* Boswell's "Life of Johnson."

turned into an asylum for the maimed and halt—
and who does not know what Macaulay calls that
strange menagerie of his in Bolt Court? He was
excellent in all the relations of life. He was an
affectionate and dutiful son, a faithful and tender
husband; what he would have been as a father we
may judge by his conduct to the children of others.
As a citizen he discharged punctiliously all his
duties; he heartily and loyally supported that
party in politics to which he attached himself and
which he believed to be in the right. When the
Government tried to corrupt him, pauper though
he was, he sternly showed its emissary the door.
His religious duties he scrupulously fulfilled
publicly and privately. To his many friends he
was helpful and loyal, and they rewarded him with
an affection such as few men have inspired. Of
his conduct to his fellow-citizens generally we
need no further testimony than what he did for
Dr. Dodd and what Goldsmith said of him—
that to be miserable was to have a natural claim
on Johnson.

And now let us briefly review the career of our
hero before we come to the most important part
of our subject—his wit and wisdom. His life falls
naturally into two eras, from 1709 to his getting
his pension and meeting with Boswell in 1762–3,
and from that point to his death in 1784. We
may call the first *Johnson as a Writer*, because
he then produced by far the greater portion of
his literary works and all the most important ones
except the "Lives of the Poets"; and the second
we may call *Johnson as a Talker*, because, as

he had now got his pension, he was relieved from what he always regarded as simple drudgery, literary composition. " I should have thought," a lady once said to him, " that as you write so well, writing must be in itself a pleasure to you." " Do you think, madam," he replied, " Leander used to swim the Hellespont for the mere pleasure of swimming ? No man but a blockhead writes except for money."

He was born at Lichfield on the 18th of September, 1709. His father, Michael Johnson, was a native of Derbyshire who married Sarah Ford, both being " well advanced in years when they married." They had two children, both sons, of whom Samuel was the elder.

In her ninetieth year Samuel Johnson thus writes to his mother :

Dear honoured mother. Neither your condition nor your character make it fit for me to say much. You have been the best mother and I believe the best woman in the world. I thank you for your indulgence to me and beg forgiveness of all that I have done ill and all that I have omitted to do well.*

In due time, after a rather severe experience of schoolmasters, who, as he said, whipped him very well, without which, as he owned, he should have done nothing, he went up to Pembroke College, Oxford. Poverty made it necessary for him to leave without a degree. Soon after this, his father having died leaving him twenty guineas, he became an usher at Market Bosworth School. But he found this employment so intolerable that he relinquished it and made his way to

* Boswell's " Life of Johnson."

Birmingham, where he completed his first prose work, a translation of Father Lolo's "Voyage to Abyssinia." The next scene is his meeting with Mrs. Porter, who confided to him that there was one objection to their match and that was that she had had an uncle who was hanged. "Oh, that," said her lover, "is of no consequence, for I have two who deserve to be hanged." Next followed an unsuccessful attempt at school-mastering at Edial, near Lichfield—the advertisement may still be read :

At Edial, near Lichfield, in Staffordshire, young gentlemen are boarded and taught the Latin and Greek languages by Samuel Johnson.*

However, only three pupils presented themselves, David Garrick, his brother Peter, and Mr. Offely. So he determined to push his fortunes in London, and the year 1737 saw him with Garrick in the city which was destined to ring with their fame.

Many years afterwards, when they were famous men dining at some great house in London, the year 1737 was mentioned.

"Ah!" said Johnson to Garrick's snobbish horror, "that was the year when I came to London with twopence halfpenny in my pocket." "Eh! what, sir," said Garrick, at Johnson's legs, "eh! what do you say, with twopence halfpenny in your pocket?" "Why yes," continued Johnson, "when I came with twopence halfpenny in *my* pocket and thou, Davy, with three halfpence in thine." *

On betaking himself to a publisher, one Wilcox, and telling him that he wished to take to litera-ture, Wilcox, eyeing the young man's sturdy

* Boswell's " Life of Johnson."

frame and broad shoulders, said, " You had better buy a porter's knot." And it was sensible advice. He arrived in London at a terrible time for authors by profession—at the very worst time known in our literary history.

His " London " was published in May 1738, appearing on the same morning as Pope's satire " 1738," "so that England had at once its Juvenal and Horace."

His " Life of Richard Savage " appeared in 1744.

In 1747 his proposal for the Dictionary was announced, the " Plan " being addressed to Lord Chesterfield.

" The Vanity of Human Wishes," which may be called the noblest moral poem extant, appeared in 1749.

Then came his tragedy " Irene," which was not produced without a violent dispute between the author and Garrick, then manager of Drury Lane Theatre, about certain changes. Johnson remarked on this :

" Sir, the fellow wants me to make ' Mahomet ' run mad that he may have an opportunity of tossing his hands and kicking his heels." *

The first issue of the *Rambler* was published on the 20th of March, 1750, and was continued till 1752. In the latter year his wife died. She had not been a good wife to him—by general consent she seems to have been quite without any charm, vulgar, coarse, and selfish—yet he wreathed her,

* Boswell's " Life of Johnson."

c

living and dead, with romantic sentiment: her memory was an open wound all his life, and he never, we are told, referred to her without tears in his eyes. Two years afterwards appeared the great Dictionary, but he made nothing by it—all the profits had been exhausted.

" I am sorry," said Boswell, " you did not get more for your Dictionary." " I am sorry too," he replied. " But it was very well. The booksellers are generous, liberal-minded men." *

Very generous and liberal-minded—when they made fortunes out of it, not one penny of which came to Johnson !

So on went this cruel drudgery. In March 1759 he wrote " Rasselas " to defray the expenses of his beloved mother's funeral and to pay some small debts she had left.

Now came a great change for him. In 1762 he was granted a pension, which he accepted. It is of interest to remark that in his Dictionary he had defined a pension as

An allowance made to any one without an equivalent. In England it is generally understood to mean pay given to a state hireling for treason to his country.

Less than a year afterwards he first met Boswell. Let Boswell tell the story :

On Monday, 16th of May, 1763, when I was sitting in Mr. Davies' back-parlour after having drunk tea with him and Mrs. Davies, Johnson unexpectedly came into the shop ; and Mr. Davies having perceived him through the glass-door in the room in which we were sitting, advancing towards us—he announced his awful approach to me somewhat in the manner of

---

* Boswell's " Life of Johnson."

an actor in the part of *Horatio* when he addresses *Hamlet* on the appearance of his father's ghost, " Look, my Lord, it comes ! " ... Mr. Davies mentioned my name and respectfully introduced me to him. I was much agitated, and recollecting his prejudice against the Scotch I said to Davies, " Don't tell where I come from." " From Scotland," cried Davies, roguishly. " Mr. Johnson, I do indeed come from Scotland, but I cannot help it." .. " That, sir, is what I find a great many of your countrymen cannot help." *

So commenced that memorable friendship which was to *make* one of them immortal, to add another title to immortality to the other, and to confer on mankind a greater boon than any other friendship in the world has conferred.

The principal incidents in Johnson's life between the meeting with Boswell and his death in 1784 may be briefly summarised. His time was principally passed in visiting his friends, in seeing the world, in social recreation—the constant attempt, as he called it, to escape from himself, in kindly and charitable actions and in talking as no mortal has ever talked since Socrates. One of his spheres was the Literary Club, founded in 1764. And here he was king, and over what subjects ! Burke, Gibbon, Reynolds, Goldsmith, Garrick, the Wartons, Fox, Dr. Percy, the flower of the literature and fashion of those times. They met at the Turk's Head in Gerrard Street, Soho, one evening in every week at seven to—any time.

In 1765 he made the acquaintance of the Thrales, and he soon had an apartment at the Brewery in Southwark and an apartment at their pleasant villa at Streatham. Then there was that

* Boswell's " Life of Johnson."

strange home of his in Fleet Street, comprised of
Mrs. Anna Williams, blind and poor, and with a
temper, we are told, marked with the Welsh fire;
Miss Polly Desmoulins, a poverty-stricken, destitute damsel whose family he had known in
Staffordshire; another destitute damsel named
Miss Carmichael; an old, semi-quack doctor
named Levett; Frank, a negro servant whom
he had rescued from the press-gang—all of whom
lived on his charity and worried his life out.
For, as he says in one of his letters :

> Williams hates everybody : Levett hates Desmoulins, and
> does not love Williams : Desmoulins hates them both. Poll loves
> none of them.*

Poll, it may be observed, was particularly trying.

> "I took to Poll," he said to Mrs. Thrale, "very well at first,
> but she won't do upon a nearer examination. We could spare
> her very well from us. Poll is a stupid slut. I *had* some hopes
> of her at first, but when I talked to her tightly and closely I could
> make nothing of her : she was wiggle waggle and I could never
> persuade her to be categorical." †

However, though there was much malice, as he
says in another letter, there was no mischief—and
so they managed to rub on together. Another of
his haunts was the Mitre, to which he used to
make his escape when feud waxed uncomfortably
warm at home.

A tour to the Hebrides in 1773—which produced two delightful works, one by himself and
one by Boswell—a visit to Paris, a visit to Wales,
and various jaunts to different places in England

* Boswell's "Life of Johnson."　　　　† Ibid.

diversified his town life.   In 1775 the University
of Oxford conferred on him the title by which we
all know him—the title of doctor.

His literary works during this period were an
edition of Shakespeare, which has certainly not
added to his reputation ; a few political pamphlets, all on the High Tory and wrong side ; and
the best of his prose works—the immortal " Lives
of the Poets." In 1783 came the signal that his
days on earth were numbered, and it is gratifying
to know that when this truly great and good man
was actually in the presence of the dread power
whom he had always regarded with so much terror
and horror, he became perfectly tranquil and
resigned ; his last articulate words were, like those
of Sir Walter Scott, a blessing : " God bless you,
my dear," and so, on the evening of the 13th of
December, 1784, Samuel Johnson ceased to be
mortal.

The great characteristic of Johnson is that he
was the most English of Englishmen, a purely
native and indigenous product, illustrating in their
most emphatic, we may almost say exaggerated,
expression the virtues as well as the defects of
the English genius, temper, and character. And
this it is which has always made him so great a
favourite with his countrymen, and so little
appreciated and relished by foreigners. Truthfulness and honesty, abomination of cant and
pretence and what the Germans so happily call
Vermessenheit, a man's mismeasurement of himself ; moral and physical courage ; *manliness*, and
contempt unutterable for the meannesses and

paltrinesses of life—and yet all this tempered, not
with a generous allowance for human frailty, but
with the good nature that has its origin in a large,
tender heart.

" My dear sir," he once said to Boswell, " clear your *mind* of
cant. You may *talk* as other people do. You may say to a man,
' Sir, I am your most humble servant.' You are *not* his most
humble servant. You may say, ' These are bad times ; it's a
melancholy thing to be reserved to such times.' You don't mind
the times. You tell a man, ' I am sorry you had such bad weather
the last day of your journey and were so much wet.' You don't
care sixpence whether he is wet or dry. You may *talk* in this
manner ; it is a mode of talking in society : but don't *think*
foolishly." *

So the abrupt way in which he declined to be
praised for a virtue to which he didn't think he
was entitled. He had been relating something
he had done. "That, sir," said Boswell, "was
great fortitude of mind." " No, sir," said Johnson, " stark insensibility." So a lady, thinking
that of course he had some ingenious explanation
to give, said to him, " Dr. Johnson, what makes
you in your Dictionary define the pastern of a
horse as ' the knee ' ? " " Pure ignorance, madam,
pure ignorance ! " was the unexpected reply.
When some of the pious friends of Dr. Dodd were
trying to console the unhappy man just before his
execution by saying that he was going to leave a
" wretched world," Johnson praised him for
having honesty enough not to join in the cant,
saying, " No, no, it has been a very agreeable
world to me." On the same account he distrusted

* Boswell's " Life of Johnson."

what we may call emotional virtues, that mere æsthetic sensibility which too often effervesces into nothing.

" I told him," says Boswell, when they had been listening to a song, " Let ambition fire thy mind," " that it affected me to such a degree as often to agitate my nerves painfully, producing in my mind alternate sensations of pathetic dejection so that I was ready to shed tears ; and of daring resolution so that I was inclined to rush into the thickest part of the battle." " Sir," said Johnson, " I should never hear it, if it made me such a fool." *

In a remark which he made on another occasion we have an admirable commentary on this unconscious form of insincerity :

" Do not, sir, accustom yourself to trust to *impressions*. There is a middle state of mind between conviction and hypocrisy of which many are conscious. By trusting to impressions a man may gradually come to yield to them, and at length be subject to them, so as not to be a free agent, or what is the same thing in effect, to *suppose* that he is not a free agent. A man who is in that state should not be suffered to live : if he declares he cannot help acting in a particular way and is irresistibly impelled, there can be no confidence in him, no more than in a tiger." †

How profoundly true ! What type of character is so absolutely hopeless as the purely emotional or æsthetic !

But if he was English in these respects, he was English in his limitations, in his strong prejudices and political bigotry. And yet I think we may say that at bottom he was far more tolerant and liberal than is commonly supposed. What could be broader or more liberal than this—with respect to religion :

" For my part, sir, I think all Christians, whether Papists or

---

* Boswell's " Life of Johnson."   † Ibid.

Protestants, agree in the essential articles, and that their differences are trivial and rather political than religious." *

And again :

" Let us not be found, when our Master calls us, ripping the lace off our waistcoats, but the spirit of contention from our souls and tongues. . . . Alas, sir, a man who cannot get to Heaven in a green coat, will not find his way thither sooner in a grey one." †

How admirable too is his remark about a man choosing a party in politics :

" I can see that a man may do right to stick to a party ; that is to say, he is a Whig or he is a Tory, and he thinks that one of those parties upon the whole the best and that to make it prevail it must be generally supported, though in particulars it may be wrong. He takes its faggot of principles in which there are fewer rotten sticks than in the other, though some rotten sticks to be sure ; and they cannot well be separated. But to bind oneself to one man or one set of men (who may be right to-day and wrong to-morrow) without any general preference of system I must disapprove." ‡

But it must be admitted that it was only in his higher moods that he talked like this ; his general tone was quite otherwise. " A Whig dog," " A Whig blockhead," " A Whig scoundrel "—were expressions only too frequently on his lips. Mrs. Knowles, not hearing him distinctly, once asked him if he had called some one a prig. Johnson : " Worse, madam ; a Whig ! But he is both." It was not often that Johnson met his match, but he did once. To Dr. Crowe at Oxford he once asked :

" Who was the first Whig ? Don't know. I see, sir, that you

---

* Boswell's " Life of Johnson."
† Piozzi's " Anecdotes of Johnson."
‡ Boswell's " Tour to the Hebrides."

are ignorant of the head of your own party, but I will tell you, sir, the Devil was the first Whig ; he wanted to set up a reform even in Heaven." Dr. Crowe : " I am much obliged to you for your information ; I certainly did not think that you would go so far back for your information, yet I rather fear that your argument makes against yourself ; for if the Devil was a Whig you have admitted that while he was a Whig he was in Heaven, but you have forgotten that the moment he got into the other place—he set up for a Tory." *

Dr. Johnson was silent for the rest of the evening. But of all his unreasonable prejudices, that against the Scotch was strongest. One night at some party a Mr. Ogilvie was dilating on the glories of Scotland. He had been rather roughly treated by Goldsmith when he got on the richness of its land, so he shifted his ground and took his stand on what he called its many noble wild prospects. The company observed unmistakable ominous symptoms in Johnson, whose head was shaking, body moving to and fro, hands vigorously rubbing his knee, while various sounds, sometimes as of the clucking of a hen and sometimes as of a half whistle, were proceeding from his mouth. At last he broke out :

" I believe, sir, you have a great many noble wild prospects. Norway, too, has noble wild prospects, and Lapland is remarkable for prodigious noble wild prospects. But, sir, let me tell you the noblest prospect which a Scotchman ever sees is the high road that leads him to England ! " †

Weaknesses of course they were ; but the dear old Doctor's very foibles endear him to us.

* I have been unable to trace the source of this story.
† Boswell's " Life of Johnson."

Sound, masculine common-sense, shrewd and penetrating, moving within a somewhat limited sphere it is true, but within that sphere irresistible because of the trenchant, incisive incisiveness with which it was expressed, is perhaps the most striking of his intellectual attributes. How often he pierces into the very core of a thing. Thus when Boswell, pointing to a splendid and sumptuous country-house, observed how happy the proprietor *must* be: "Nay, sir," said Johnson, "all this excludes but *one* evil—poverty." Again, speaking of the *importance of trifles :*

"Pound St. Paul's Church into atoms, and consider any single atom ; it is, to be sure, good for nothing ; but put all these atoms together and you have St. Paul's Church. So it is with human felicity, which is made up of many ingredients, each of which may be shown to be very insignificant." *

Take again this about suicide :

"Suppose, sir," said Boswell, "that a man is absolutely sure that if he lives a few days longer he will be detected in fraud, the consequence of which will be utter disgrace and expulsion from society." "Then, sir," replied the sage, "let him go abroad to a distant country, let him go to some place where he is *not* known. Don't let him go to the Devil where he *is* known." †

So in his remark about gambling or gaming :

"Gaming is a mode of transferring property without producing any intermediate good." ‡

Take again his shrewd common-sense :

I talked of the mode adopted by some to rise in the world by courting great men, and asked him whether he had ever submitted

---

* Boswell's " Life of Johnson."
† Boswell's " Tour to the Hebrides."
‡ Boswell's " Life of Johnson."

to it. " Why, sir, I never was near enough to great men to court them. You may be prudently attached to great men and yet independent. You are not to do what you think wrong, and you are to calculate and not pay too dear for what you get. You must not give a shilling's worth of court for sixpence worth of good. But if you can get a shilling's worth of good for sixpence worth of court, you are a fool if you do not pay court." *

How well he knew human nature ! Take his instantaneous solution of Goldsmith's popularity in society. After he had observed that it was amazing how little Goldsmith knew and that he seldom went where he was not more ignorant than any one else in the company :

" Yet," said Sir Joshua Reynolds, " there is no man whose company is more liked." " To be sure, sir," was the reply. " When people find a man of the most distinguished abilities as a writer their inferior while he is with them, it must be highly gratifying to them." †

Again :

" A man should be careful never to tell tales of himself to his own disadvantage. People may be amused, laugh at the time, but they will be remembered and brought up against him upon some subsequent occasion." ‡

On another occasion Boswell, to start a question, asked whether when a man knows that some of his intimate friends are invited to the house of another friend, with whom they are all equally intimate, he may join them without an invitation :

" No, sir, he is not to go when he is not invited. They may be invited on purpose to abuse him."

How excellent, too, is his remark upon the difference between a well-bred and ill-bred man :

* Boswell's " Life of Johnson."   † Ibid.   ‡ Ibid.

" One," he said, " immediately attracts your liking, the other your aversion. You love the one till you find reason to hate him : you hate the other till you find reason to love him." *

We do not usually associate the idea of what we call good-breeding with Johnson, and yet it is remarkable that he exemplified it to the point of refined subtlety.

When Johnson was asked whether he made any reply to a very high compliment which the King paid him, he replied :

" No, sir, when the King had said it, it was to be so. It was not for me to bandy civilities with my sovereign." †

Another point which characterised Johnson was his extraordinary readiness in repartee. Sir Joshua Reynolds remarked that there was no flourishing with his sword, that he was through you in a moment. " Oh, surely, sir," said Boswell of Mrs. Montague's work on Shakespeare—" it is a work which does her honour." " Yes, sir, it does *her* honour, but it would do nobody else honour." " Dr. Johnson, do you advise me to marry ? " said a young man who appears to have been worrying him with what he detested— direct question. " Sir," replied the sage, " I advise no man to marry who is not likely to propagate understanding." ‡ When the last instalment of the Dictionary was over he got this etter from Andrew Millar the publisher :

Andrew Millar sends his compliments to Mr. Samuel Johnson

---

* Boswell's " Life of Johnson."   † Ibid.
‡ Piozzi's " Anecdotes of Johnson."

with the money for the last sheet of the dictionary and thanks God he has done with him.

The reply he got by return was :

Samuel Johnson returns his compliments to Mr. Andrew Millar and is very glad to find, as he does by his note, that Andrew Millar has the grace to thank God for anything.*

Take the following lively passage :

Johnson : "To talk of *respect* for a *player!*" Boswell : "There, sir, you are always heretical; you never will allow merit to a player." Johnson : "Merit, sir—what merit ? Do you respect a rope-dancer or a ballad singer ? " Boswell : "No, sir, but we respect a great player, as a man who can conceive lofty sentiments and can express them gracefully." Johnson : "What, sir, a fellow who claps a hump on his back and a lump on his leg and cries, 'I am Richard III.' Nay, sir, a ballad singer is a higher man, for he does two things : he repeats and he sings . . . the player only recites." Boswell : "My dear sir, you may turn anything into ridicule . . . a great player does what very few people are capable to do : his art is a very rare faculty. *Who* can repeat Hamlet's soliloquy as Garrick does it ? " Johnson : "Anybody may ; Jemmy there "—pointing to a boy about eight years old who was in the room—"will do it as well in a week." Boswell : "No, no, sir, and as a proof of the merit of great acting and of the value which mankind sets upon it, Garrick has got £100,000." Johnson : "Is getting £100,000 a proof of excellence ? That has been done by a scoundrel commissary." †

Well might poor Boswell say, "This was most fallacious reasoning." "I have found you an argument, sir," he once said to a man who was still taking exception ; "I am not obliged to find you

* Hawkins' "Life of Johnson." Boswell gives a different version of this story, the message being delivered by word of mouth.

† Boswell's "Life of Johnson."

an understanding." Nothing irritated him more than people attempting to defend what was vicious and mischievous. Thus a gentleman was once defending drinking, adding to his other arguments this : " You know, sir, drinking drives away care and makes us forget whatever is disagreeable. Would not you allow a man to drink for that reason ? " " Yes, sir," was the reply, " if he sat next you."

He had an inimitable knack of insinuating sarcasm where it was not directly expressed, as where he said of the Irish, " The Irish are a FAIR PEOPLE, they never speak well of one another." So, too, in his remark to Boswell, who had made, as was too common with that gentleman, one of his indiscreet confidences :

One day I owned to him that " I was occasionally troubled with a fit of *narrowness*." " Why, sir," said he, " so am I—*but I do not tell it*." *

A gentleman had once quitted a party where Johnson was, and the company were speculating as to who he was and what was his profession. The Doctor observed that " he did not care to speak ill of any man behind his back, but he believed the gentleman was an *attorney*." So, too, on a certain occasion a gentleman introduced his brother to the Doctor, this said brother being presumably a rather dull-looking man. " When we have sat together some time, Dr. Johnson, you'll find my brother grow very entertaining." " Sir," said Johnson, " I can wait."

* Boswell's " Life of Johnson."

How witty, too, his illustrations sometimes are, as when he said on being told of some women preaching :

"Sir, a woman's preaching is like a dog's walking on his hind legs. It is not done well, but you are surprised to find it done at all." *

Again, on hearing of a gentleman who had been very unhappy in marriage, marrying immediately after his wife died, Johnson observed that it was the triumph of hope over experience. A very conceited, empty-headed fellow once met Johnson and lamented that he had lost all his Greek. "I believe it happened at the same time, sir," said Johnson, "that I lost all my large estate in Yorkshire." †

It has been sometimes said that Johnson is now forgotten as a writer and lives only in the pages of Boswell as a conversationalist ; if this be so it is our misfortune and not his. Perhaps he is more attractive as a talker than as a writer because the stateliness, not to say pomposity, of his style is not to the taste of these days and is, it must be admitted, somewhat wearisome. But his works form a most important and precious contribution to English literature. His papers in the *Rambler*, the *Idler*, and the *Adventurer* are full of good things, great moral truths, penetrating remarks on life and men and books.

His prefaces to his Dictionary and his Shakespeare are, as compositions, noble pieces. His "Rasselas" does not present a very cheerful view of

* Boswell's "Life of Johnson."
† Piozzi's "Anecdotes of Johnson."

life, it must be admitted—we should remember
the circumstances under which it was written—
but it is one of the weightiest and wisest of moral
tales. Of the " Lives of the Poets " it would be
no exaggeration to say that, with all its defects,
some of them very serious, it holds one of the
very first places in English critical literature.
As a poet Johnson has produced two masterpieces—"London" and "The Vanity of Human
Wishes," the latter perhaps the noblest moral
poem in our literature, and indeed challenging
the supremacy of the superb poem * of Juvenal's
on which it is modelled.

In conclusion, few men who have ever lived are so
well worth knowing intimately as Samuel Johnson
—as the Socrates of Fleet Street, especially in
these days. It is our lot to be living in an age
when many of us, perhaps most of us, don't well
know where we are, so busy everywhere is the
spirit of transition, so bewildering the revolution
which seems to be changing the face of everything.
But here was a man who knew where he was, and
spoke with no uncertain voice. As every age has
its own needs, moral and spiritual, so every age
creates its own teachers; and Johnson is very far
indeed from being able to supply us with everything we require in the way of guidance and
admonition; but we can go to him for much which
every age must require, and should be grateful
for: a noble example of self-subjugation, of
heroic endurance, of duties faithfully fulfilled, of
honesty, sincerity, humanity. All that common-

* Tenth Satire.

sense and mother wit in unusual measure, immense information, ample experience of men and life tempered with a reverent and pious spirit, can under their time-limitation teach us shall we learn from him. If mere amusement and recreation be our object, what book in the world since Plutarch's "Lives" can match with the work in which Boswell tells Johnson's story— that Odyssey, as it has been called, of the eighteenth century? No man in that or in any other age of our literature has such a charm, such a singular attraction for us. In intellectual power, in grasp, fertility, and eloquence, Burke was undoubtedly his superior; in mere learning he was no match for Gibbon; in charm of style no match for Goldsmith; but they have not got hold of us as he has done, they have not his commanding personality—they have not his character. And the last few years have shown that his fame, so far from decreasing, is growing still—have shown that Mr. Austin Dobson's words do but express what all of us who love and admire the dear old Doctor will echo lustily back:

You may talk of your BURKES and your GIBBONS so clever,
But I hark back to him with a "JOHNSON for ever!"
And I feel as I muse on his ponderous figure,
Though he's great in this age, in the next he'll grow bigger.*

---

* A Postscript to "Retaliation."

EDMUND BURKE

THE two most pathetic figures in political history are two of the greatest men who have adorned it, Demosthenes and Burke. Both, animated by the purest motives, patriots to the innermost fibre, with no thought, with no aim but for the public good, wore out their lives in leading forlorn hopes and in fighting losing battles. Both were prophets with the curse of Cassandra upon them, to be found wise after the event, to be believed when all was lost. Who can read the " Philippics " and " Olynthiacs," who can read the speeches on American Taxation and on Conciliation with America, without indignant astonishment at the stupidity and supineness of those whom such irresistible logic could not convince, such over-powering eloquence arouse ? But Demosthenes saw Athens at the feet of a Macedonian despot, and Burke saw England dismembered of America and at war with half the world. Of the super-human efforts made by the great Athenian to retrieve the disasters in which the neglect of his warnings had involved his countrymen, there was not one which was not thwarted either by a cruel fortune or by the perfidy and levity of those whom he was striving in their own despite to save. Burke's failures and baffled virtues resulted in less tragical issues, it is true, but they

must have been equally mortifying and grievous.
To frame measures and propose schemes the
nobleness and luminous wisdom of which posterity
was to discover, and to see them ignored or
defeated by corrupt and selfish factions and by
his own timid colleagues; to address to empty
benches masterpieces of political wisdom eloquent
with an eloquence the like of which mankind had
never heard since Cicero; to be the one man
who solved correctly almost every political
problem of his time, only to find himself de-
nounced as a visionary and fanatic—such was
Burke's experience of public life. On the losing
side in every important action of his life, he was
on the losing side to the last, perishing miserably
amid the ruins of his party and the wreck of his
hopes. If the closing scene in the life of Demosthenes is more awfully impressive, it is scarcely
more pathetic than the scene on which the
curtain fell at Beaconsfield. History has done
justice to Demosthenes, it has not done justice
to Burke. The Whigs have never forgiven him
for creating a schism in the party, and have
availed themselves of his grave errors with regard
to certain aspects of the Revolution to represent
him, if they wish to speak tenderly of him, as a
madman; if they wish to speak harshly, as an
apostate. But he was neither a madman nor an
apostate. He was a very wise and a very honest
man. Assuming as he did that the Revolution
on the Continent was a precedent for a similar
revolution in England and that what was at stake
was nothing less than the whole fabric of our

social and political system, he was perfectly justified in taking—it was imperative on him as a patriot to take—the course he did. Once taken and the fire kindled in him, the rest followed. He never deserted his party: his party deserted him.

Of all the charges which have been brought against Burke the most baseless is the charge of inconsistency. Lord Brougham has said that it would be difficult to select one leading principle or prevailing sentiment in Burke's later writings to which something extremely adverse may not be found in his former. It may be at once conceded that on a superficial view of Burke's attitude towards the constitutional struggle of which Wilkes was the centre, towards the American Revolution, and towards Economical Reform, and of his attitude towards the Revolution in France and the revolutionary party in England, there seems much to justify the charge. It would be very easy to marshal an array of sentiments and opinions drawn from the "Thoughts on the . . . Present Discontents," the American speeches, and the speech on Economical Reform against an array of sentiments and opinions culled from the " Reflections " and the " Letters on a Regicide Peace," and ask triumphantly in what way they can be reconciled. It would be easy to point out that in 1772 he supported a Bill for granting the Dissenters privileges from which they were excluded by the Test Act, and that in 1790 he opposed a Bill granting them those privileges. But if we look a little carefully into them we shall find that these seeming inconsistencies are easily reconciled, that Burke's political creed in 1796 was precisely what it was in 1771, that it had changed in no article whatever. What had changed were circumstances, and the change in Burke was no change in principles and tenets, but in the part he was forced to play—the attitude he was compelled to assume for the conservation of those tenets and principles.

A short sketch of his career * till the breaking out of the Revolution will help us to understand how much of a piece that part of his life and conduct which those who taunt him with apostasy deplore and execrate, and excuse only on the ground that he had become half-insane, was with that part of it to which they point with pride and gratitude. Few men have entered public life so admirably equipped for its duties and so peculiarly predisposed, both by circumstances and training, to approach it in a large and liberal spirit. With his father a Protestant, his mother a Roman Catholic, and his first teacher a Quaker, he was not only entirely free from religious prejudices but, what was more important, had had it early brought home to him that truth, and fruitful truth, has many sides. These early surroundings certainly go far to account for one of Burke's most striking characteristics — his flexible and hospitable mind. The variety of his studies at Trinity College, Dublin, and the

* He was born at Dublin probably in 1729, but even the year of his birth is uncertain.

ardour with which he pursued them we all know
—how at one time he devoted himself to mathematics and had his *furor mathematicus ;* then betook himself to logic, till the *furor logicus* yielded
to a passionate devotion to history; the *furor
historicus* yielded in its turn to the *furor poeticus.*
Leaving Trinity College with immense stores of
the most varied acquirements, having indeed
surveyed, within the measure of a youth's
capacity, almost the whole area of learning, he
betook himself to London. There his literary
occupations—among them the political survey of
Europe in the " Annual Register," and a " History
of the American Settlement," as well as his duties
and opportunities while in the service of William
Gerard Hamilton—were of invaluable service to
him in his political education. In the year
1765 he was, by the influence of Lord Verney,
returned to Parliament for the borough of
Wendover. The party to which he attached
himself and in the cause of which he laboured so
long as it retained its identity was the party led
by the Marquis of Rockingham. It was a party
distinguished by its integrity, its disinterestedness,
its moderation, and its consistency during a time
of almost unexampled political profligacy and
incompetence. It was the party which retained
in their purity the principles of that great Whig
party which had brought about the Revolution of
1688: with those principles it never paltered.
It upheld them while the subserviency of a selfish
faction to an obstinate and tyrannical king and
the feuds and dissensions of what should have

constituted the opposition to this tyranny imperilled our liberties, lost us America, and brought
us to the lowest point of national depression. It
upheld them when a third power, called into being
by the natural course of progress and into
importance through being made the counters
with which these factions played their game—
namely, what is now known as the democracy—
was threatening to turn the scale to the opposite
extreme. The Ark of the Covenant of this party
was the Constitution of 1688, their aim the
maintenance of a due equipoise between the
principles represented by monarchy, aristocracy,
and democracy. But we must guard carefully
against attaching to democracy the sense it bears
now. The "people" were then, politically speaking, non-existent and were absolutely unrepre-
sented, having no share at all in the direction of
affairs ; in fact, democracy in our sense of the
term was an unknown quantity in the Constitution
of 1688. The democratic element was represented by the Commons, and the Commons were,
as political agents, the nominees either of the
Crown or of the aristocracy and great landed
classes, or members of these last bodies. It
would be a great mistake to associate Burke at any
period of his career with democratic ideas. The
only parliamentary reform he and his party ever
contemplated was to readjust the balance in the
Commons between the representatives of the
aristocracy and the representatives of the Crown—
a balance which was then overwhelmingly pre-
ponderant on the Crown's side—and to infuse,

but very cautiously, an element representing the interests of the great mercantile classes. His Ark of the Covenant was, let me repeat, the Constitution of 1688. That was his ideal: on the preservation of that depended, in his belief, the safety, the prosperity, the glory of the English nation.

This places us in the very centre of Burke's political ideals, explains his motives of action, and enables us to reconcile his policy and position between 1790 and 1796 with his policy and position between 1765 and 1789. As the Constitution which he so nobly describes had been the result of compromise, of a cautious and sober adjustment of the principles of prescription to the principles of progress; as it combined the results of purified experiment with the results of a spirit of reverent conservatism, so it became ideally, as he himself has said, a sort of Bible to him. And a Bible in a double sense—a Bible which he believed contained the gospel of England's political salvation, and a Bible out of which he derived the teaching which guided his actions and moulded and coloured the whole of his public conduct and policy. If we look at all the chief events with which he was associated before the breaking out of the Revolution and note the part he played in them, we observe the same prudent moderation, the same spirit of compromise. Thus, with regard to the American Revolution, he upheld the imperial authority and maintained the right of England to tax, but deprecated the exercise of that right on the ground of inexpediency. Thus he was wholly in favour of relaxing the commercial and legislative restriction on the Anglo-Irish, and even lost his seat in supporting a Bill in favour of alleviation; but though he tried to educate his party on the Irish question, he never pressed the matter further. Thus he at first supported Clarkson in his crusade against the slave-trade, but abandoned the attempt for fear of injuring his party by alienating the West Indian interest. Then he opposed Parliamentary Reform on the ground that it would lessen the power of those orders in the State who had the greatest stake in the country. Thus in 1790 he refused the Dissenters the relief he had been willing to give them in 1772 because the time was not propitious to such indulgence. The same moderation marked his scheme for Economical Reform. He resisted all attempts which involved radical changes in any essential part of the Constitution. " I heave," he said, " the lead every inch of the way I make." In his Notes on the Amendment to the Address, 1774, he has a typical passage :

Nothing is more beautiful in the theory of Parliaments than that principle of renovation and union, of permanency and change that are happily mixed in their constitution ; that in all our changes we are never wholly old or wholly new : that there are enough of the old to preserve unbroken the traditional chain of the maxims and policy of our ancestors and the law and custom of Parliament, and enough of the new to invigorate us and bring us to our true character by being taken from the mass of the people : and the whole, though mostly composed of the old members, have, notwithstanding, a new character and may have the advantage of change without the imputation of inconstancy.

He says in another place:

The old building stands well enough, though part Gothic, part Grecian, and part Chinese, until an attempt is made to square it into uniformity. Then indeed it may come down upon our heads all together in much conformity of ruin: and great will be the fall thereof.

But he has no objection to modification, and he would have the fabric elastic, for a State without the means of change is without the means of its conservation. His political philosophy is penetrated with the same spirit: it is of the essence of compromise: its criteria are the possible, the expedient, the becoming: it is not concerned with abstract principles except in their bounded application to facts and circumstances.

Circumstances [he writes] give in reality to every political principle its distinguishing colour and discriminating effect. The circumstances are what render every civil and political scheme beneficial or obnoxious to mankind.†

As Mr. Payne has observed, what a German metaphysical theologian at the end of the last century, after many wearisome attempts to square religion with abstract principles, observed of Christianity, *Das Christenthum ist keine Philosophie*, may be exactly applied to Burke's conception of politics, *Die Politik ist keine Philosophie*. It is purely empirical, not a matter of rules and ideas but of observation and practice: it is a computing principle: what it has to deal with are differences of good, are compromises some-

* "Observations on the Present State of the Nation."
† "Reflections on the French Revolution."

times between good and evil, sometimes between evil and evil—for it works " standing on earth, not rapt above the pole." Hence his defence of party in answer to the rhodomontade of Bolingbroke, and his constant insistence on the necessity of fidelity to party interests at almost any cost, except when issues of important moment to the welfare of mankind are imperilled.

> I can see [said his friend Dr. Johnson] that a man may do right to stick to a party ; that is to say, he is a Whig or he is a Tory, and he thinks that one of those parties upon the whole the best and that to make it prevail it must be generally supported, though in particulars it may be wrong. He takes its faggot of principles in which there are fewer rotten sticks than in the other, though some rotten sticks to be sure, and they cannot well be separated.*

This was exactly Burke's view, and in Rockingham's party, in its faggot principles and aims, there were certainly far fewer rotten sticks than in the faggot of any other party in Burke's time. It is not, he contended, a question whether monarchy, whether oligarchy, whether democracy are in themselves desirable, but whether in their purity or their combination they are fitted to the needs of a particular community. Thus he argued of the Revolution that if a great change were to be made in human affairs the minds of men would be fitted to it : the general opinions and feelings would draw that way ; and that those who persisted in opposing this mighty current in human affairs would appear rather to resist the decrees of Providence itself than the mere designs of men. The late Lord Coleridge once said to

* Boswell's " Tour to the Hebrides."

a friend of mine, an enthusiastic young barrister,
" You cannot greatly help justice till you have
ceased greatly to care for her." This was putting
it a little cynically, but it exactly indicates
Burke's conception of the relation of abstract
ideals to the possibility of what can be realised.
He had as little confidence as Bishop Butler in
the perfectibility either of man or of the world.
Facts are facts, and they must be confronted.
He had no sympathy with the democracy, and
yet he wrote :

In all disputes between them [the people] and their rulers,
the presumption is at least upon a par in favour of the people. . . .
The people have no interest in disorder.*

So with respect to the American colonists he said :

The question with me is, not whether you have a right to
render your people miserable ; but whether it is not your interest
to make them happy. †

And again :

I do not know the method of drawing up an indictment
against a whole people. ‡

In temper and constitution Burke was one of
the noblest men who ever lived, a patriot as pure
as Hampden and Washington, a philanthropist as
ardent as Howard and Clarkson, as passionate a
lover of liberty, justice, and light, as passionate a
hater of all that impeded them, as any man who
has ever been in the van of aspiring humanity, as

* " Thoughts on the Cause of the Present Discontents."
† " Speech on Conciliation with America."
‡ Ibid.

his career between 1765 and 1789 shows, and
shows conclusively. But his sagacity and practical
wisdom, his knowledge of human nature and of
the conditions and laws under which life moves
and men work, kept all this from wasting itself
either in Quixotic action or in Quixotic speech.
"I pitched," he said, referring to the outset
of his political life, "my ideas of liberty low
that they might stick to me and that I might
stick to them to the end of my life." No man
was ever more free from Utopian delusions. No
man ever so shy of drawing bills on hope for
experience to discount. What had actually been
achievable and what was demonstrably possible
bounded the horizon of his political sympathies
and of his political aspirations. It is in such
passages as the peroration of his speech on Conciliation with America that his greatness is seen.
Here burst into flame and blaze—for they could
serve occasion—the patriotism, the philanthropy,
the love of justice, liberty, and light which ever
glowed an intense but suppressed fire within him.
Here pure reason, plain sense, and simple facts,
penetrated with passion and clad in glorious
apparel, seem like the raptures of the poet.

The Revolution found Burke in the vigour of
his genius and of his intellectual powers, but
depressed, harassed, and broken by four-and-
twenty years of almost superhuman labours. He
had failed in everything except in bringing
Warren Hastings to trial. He had seen America
torn from England, Government a chaos of
factions, his party wrecked, its remnant hurried

into follies and crimes which had first disgraced
and then proscribed it. And now the last and
saddest chapter in his troubled life was to open.

In May 1789 met the States-General. In
July of the same year the Bastille was taken. Then
followed the Declaration of the Rights of Man
and the Decree of the Fourth of August, and the
irruption of the mob into the palace of Versailles.

These events drew from Burke in November
1790 his " Reflections," though the work was
directly called forth on account of an address
given by a Dr. Richard Price, a Nonconformist
minister, to the Revolutionary Society. Contrary
to the view taken by Price, Burke fiercely
attacked the Revolution in these " Reflections "
and in his subsequent writings, viz. " Thoughts
on French Affairs " and a " Letter to a Member
of the National Assembly," in which he prophesied
the course things were certain to take:

The shifting tides of fear and hope, the flight and the pursuit,
the peril and escape, the alternate famine and feasts of the savage
and the thief, after a time render all course of slow, steady,
progressive, unvaried occupation, and the prospect only of a
limited mediocrity at the end of long labour, to the last degree
tame, languid, and insipid. . . . They will assassinate the King
when his name will no longer be necessary to their designs. . . .
They will probably first assassinate the Queen.*

Meanwhile he had set the kingdom on fire,
having previously broken with Fox and Sheridan
and split the Whig party in two. Then came out
in answer to the numerous attacks on him
" An Appeal from the New to the Old Whigs,"

* " Letter to a Member of the National Assembly."

1791, in which he demonstrates that it is not he who has changed, but they: that he remains true to the old flag—that of the true Whigs—while they have gone off into mad democrats and incendiaries to break up and ruin the noble English Constitution, the Ark of the Old Covenant. The Whigs of this day, he concludes by saying, have before them in this appeal their constitutional ancestors: they have the doctors of the modern school. They will choose for themselves. The author of the " Reflections " has chosen for himself. The " Conduct of the Minority," written two years later, is a defence of his own conduct, and an arraignment of that of Fox and his friends. Meanwhile the Revolution had been proceeding just as Burke had prophesied, horror on horror accumulating. The King had been executed, war had been declared between England and France, the Armed Coalition was melting away, England and Austria were left alone. France was in the hands of the Directory and everywhere triumphant. Fox and his party had, of course, opposed the war with France from the beginning; Pitt never loved it and was now anxious for peace with the Directory. So in 1796 Pitt opened negotiations for peace with France.

It was to oppose that peace that Burke wrote, and wrote in fire, the " Letters on a Regicide Peace," those scathing Philippics against what he called the pusillanimity and madness of England in attempting to establish friendly relations with a country which was aggressively republican and revolutionary. Identifying France with lawless-

ness and anarchy, with the principles of all that
was base and brutal, with all that was inimical to
civil order and private decency; denouncing her
as the enemy of the human race, as a common
and insufferable nuisance stinking in the nostrils
of Europe, as the blood-reeking, offal-loaded lair
of robbers, pariahs, and assassins, he conjured his
countrymen, as they valued the Constitution, as
they valued the existence of their national life and
Church, Throne, State, as they valued social order,
honour, religion, reason, decency, to have no
peace with France, not to condescend to recognise
its existence as a political unit, to expunge it from
the roll of nations, to obliterate it from the map.
In no works extant are there more magnificent
passages of sustained and fiery eloquence, invec-
tive more terrific, sarcasm more blasting, more
jewels of rhetoric and felicitous expression, nay,
and making all allowance for intemperance and
extravagance, heat and fury, more jewels of
crystallised wisdom.

They were a voice from Burke's deathbed.
They were written when he was reeling under
the blow that broke him, the death of his son,
when disease and anxiety and sorrow had bowed
and broken him.

A miserable triumph over miserable adversaries closes the scene. It was known that Burke
was on the verge of actual beggary, and Pitt pro-
cured for him a pension without bringing the
matter before Parliament. The Duke of Bedford
and Lord Lauderdale, seeing in this a weapon for
attacking Pitt, opposed the pension in the House

of Lords. The head of the house of Bedford was not quite the proper person to oppose a grant from the Crown, and in the " Letter to a Noble Lord," so justly described by Lord Morley as the most splendid repartee in the English language, Burke expresses his surprise that objection to his pension should have come from that particular quarter. For the pension was surely not altogether given without some equivalent, and was after all only a small one. But

The Duke of Bedford is the leviathan among all the creatures of the Crown. He tumbles about his unwieldy bulk : he plays and frolics in the ocean of the royal bounty. Huge as he is and whilst " he lies floating many a rood," he is still a creature. His ribs, his fins, his whalebone, his blubber, the very spiracles through which he spouts a torrent of brine against his origin, and covers me all over with the spray—everything of him and about him is from the throne. Is it for *him* to question the dispensation of the royal favour ?

Sadly the old man pointed out how more than an equivalent might have been paid for the royal bounty :

Had it pleased God to continue to me the hopes of succession, I should have been, according to my mediocrity, and the mediocrity of the age I live in, a sort of founder of a family ; I should have left a son, who in all the points in which personal merit can be viewed, in science, in erudition, in genius, in taste, in honour, in generosity, in humanity, in every liberal sentiment, and every liberal accomplishment, would not have shewn himself inferior to the Duke of Bedford, or to any of those whom he traces in his line.

Pathetic indeed, pathetic beyond expression that it should have been in the midst of feuds like

E

these—in the midst of gloom and storm like
this—with no ray of the glory that was beyond
even faintly perceptible to him, that the great
soul of this man who had laboured for England
and for mankind, always in righteousness and
sincerity, for five-and-thirty years was to take its
flight. We now know that Burke with reference
to the Revolution was a false prophet, that if he
discerned clearly the immediate consequences he
did not discern the ultimate consequences of
that stupendous convulsion: he miscalculated on
all sides: he miscalculated even ludicrously the
power of France and of those whom principles
allied with her: he confounded what was
accidental with what was essential: he did not
perceive the solidity, steadiness, and good sense
which underlay the superficial tumult and agitation in England. But let us not underrate the
value of his anti-Revolutionary writings. If we
have outgrown much which he regarded with
superstitious reverence, if the glamour with which
in his eyes sentiment invested monarchy and
aristocracy is now dimming and fading: if we are
pressing to other goals than had defined themselves to him, if experiment and experience have
justified us in feeling confidence where he
doubted and mistrusted, we should do well to
remember and find guidance in many of his
characteristic precepts and warnings—that if we
look forward to posterity we should not forget to
look backward to our ancestors, that prescription
and tradition should neither be contemptuously
ignored nor rudely violated, that what has grown

up historically can only perish historically, that
the application of abstract rights and principles
to an organisation so composite and artificial as
political society and its economy is the most
difficult and delicate of problems, that the only
sure test of political wisdom is expediency—
expediency not in the narrow and selfish, but in
the highest and most comprehensive sense of the
term.

WILLIAM GODWIN AND
MARY WOLLSTONECRAFT

IF you had dropped in at one of Lamb's
Wednesday evenings in the Temple, at
about ten o'clock P.M., you would most
probably have seen at the whist-table
a somewhat remarkable-looking man, with a
massive head altogether out of proportion to
the insignificant body which supported it, with
placid, benignant features, and with a particularly
gracious suavity of manner. Had you requested
to be introduced to him, you would have found
him a man of few words and, though plainly a
philosopher, by no means disposed to talk of
serious subjects. You would have been struck
with the delicacy and precision of expression,
bordering, you would have felt, on the finical,
with which, in the lowest of voices, he delivered
what he had to say to you. Could you have
drawn him out of his shell, you would very soon
have discovered that you were in communication
with no common intellect, but with an intellect
of steel, and steel of the ice-hook's temper, as
hard and cold as it was keen and poignant; that
neither passion nor sentiment, neither imagination
nor fancy, no touch of humour, no suspicion of
wit, had part in your strange companion's composition. Had you been a young gentleman of

68

fortune, it is more than probable that your new friend would have solicited the honour of further acquaintance with you, and would have taken an early opportunity of communicating that he was in great straits for money, and that any loan from five pounds to five hundred would just then be particularly acceptable; and you would have noticed that he requested this rather as a right than as a favour. Whatever you might have thought of him, the one thing which you would have found it difficult to realise in relation to your composed and staid companion was that he was the high priest of anarchy and the author of a work at the potential effects of which the maddest incendiary in Europe would have been appalled. Godwin presents the extraordinary anomaly, not of a philosopher among fanatics— for that is not uncommon—but of a fanatic among philosophers. Reason seems to have had the same effect on him as mere enthusiasm has on other men. What sobers most men intoxicated him. What quenches them gave him fire. At the point to which others are rapt by transporting excitement, he arrived by a cold process of mathematical calculation.

The sensation which Burke's " Reflections " made among politicians was scarcely greater than the sensation which the " Political Justice " made in inquiring philosophico-political circles. " No work in our time," said Hazlitt, " gave such a blow to the philosophical mind of this country." Tom Paine was considered for a time as Tom Fool to Godwin; Paley an old woman, Edmund

Burke a flashy sophist. Truth, moral truth had here taken up its abode and these were the oracles of thought. "It carried," said De Quincey, "one single shock into the bosom of English society, fearful but momentary, like that from the electric blow of the gymnotus." But it did not meet with the approval of many friends of the Revolution. Horne Tooke pronounced it to be "a bad book which would do a great deal of harm," and even Holcroft said "that though it was written with very good intentions, yet, to be sure, nothing could be so foolish." The poet Crabbe's remark about it was characteristic and hit it off in quiet humour. "I have never felt before, nor, I am afraid, have I ever felt since, so strongly the duty of not living to oneself, but of having for one's sole object the good of the community." But to turn to its author.

Born March 3, 1756, at Wisbeach, in Cambridgeshire, his father being a Dissenting minister at that place, he was brought up by an aunt who was a rigid Calvinist and who dinned into him the religious views of that sect. He passed next into the tuition of one Samuel Newton, a minister of the Independent Congregation at Norwich, whose creed, derived from the writings of Sandeman, had supplemented that of Calvin; for Calvin's creed having damned ninety-nine in a hundred who were not Calvinists, this creed damned ninety-nine in a hundred who were Calvinists. He had thus, at the opening of life, laid an excellent foundation for that reaction which in his thirty-first year made him an unbeliever, and in his thirty-sixth an atheist. In 1773 he entered the Dissenting College at Hoxton, where he spent five years, reading among other things all the authors for and against the Trinity, original sin, and the most disputed doctrines; but, finding his understanding not sufficiently instructed for impartial decision, all his inquiries terminated in Calvinism. He had also, he says, adopted the principles of Toryism with regard to politics. In 1778 he settled as a Dissenting minister at Ware, in Hertfordshire. But now a great change was about to come over him, for he was brought into contact with the first of the four instructors to whom he tells us he felt his mind first indebted for improvement, namely, Joseph Fawcet, Thomas Holcroft, George Dyson, and S. T. Coleridge. Fawcet, whose name is now forgotten, delivered the Sunday Evening Lectures at the Old Jewry. He had, according to Hazlitt, a singularly pure and noble character, and Hazlitt adds: " He was one of the most enthusiastic admirers of the French Revolution, and I believe that the disappointment of the hopes he had cherished of the freedom and happiness of mankind preyed upon his mind and hastened his death."

Thomas Holcroft, whom Godwin first met in 1786, and with whom two years afterwards he became on terms of brotherly intimacy, was a very remarkable man. The son of a shoe-maker, he had been successively stable-boy, shoe-maker, actor, dramatist, and novelist. Stern, irascible, and perfervid, he carried revolutionary notions to excess. " Rectitude and Courage were," said Mrs. Shelley, " the Gods of his idolatry. He would contend that death and disease existed only through the feebleness of man's mind and—happy man !—that *pain* had no reality."

In 1785 Godwin came up to London, dropped the title of Reverend, betook himself to journalism and miscellaneous literature, and threw himself into the life of the time. Then came the great event which found him an unbeliever rapidly developing into an atheist—they are his own terms—in religion, and a republican in politics.

In his diary, 1789, he writes :

This was the year of the French Revolution. My heart beat high with great swelling sentiments of Liberty. I had been for nine years, in principles, a republican. I had read with great satisfaction the writings of Rousseau, Helvetius, and others—the most popular authors in France. I observed in them a system more general and simply philosophical than in the majority of English writers on political subjects, and I could not refrain from conceiving sanguine hopes of a revolution of which such writings had been the precursors. Yet I was far from approving all that I saw even in the commencement of the revolution. . . . I never for a moment ceased to disapprove of mob government and the impulses which men, collected together in multitudes, produce on each other. I desired such political changes only as should flow purely from the clear light of the understanding and the erect and generous feelings of the heart.*

This puts comprehensively Godwin's attitude to the Revolution.

In 1793 appeared " Political Justice," which, if written in the interests of democracy, was

* C. Kegan Paul's "William Godwin."

certainly published at a very aristocratic price—
three guineas. This is said to have been the
reason that proceedings were not taken against
it by the Government, Pitt observing to the
Privy Council that a three-guinea book could
never do much harm among those who had not
three shillings to spare! Mrs. Shelley tells us,
however, that the high price her father placed
on the work was in strict conformity with his
principles. He was an advocate for improvements
brought in by the enlightened and sober-minded,
but he deprecated abrupt innovations and appeals
to the passion of the multitude. " Political
Justice " was succeeded by " Caleb Williams,"
published in 1794, designed to illustrate dramatically the doctrines inculcated in the former work,
by a general review of the modes of domestic and
unrecorded despotism by which man becomes
the destroyer of man—the hero being the victim
of autocratic power and of maladministered and
tyrannical laws.

As our business is with Godwin in direct
relation to the French Revolution, it is not
necessary to deal with his many other literary
and historical works produced between 1794 and
1834, or to enter into further details about his
private life beyond the period of his connection
with Shelley.

In January 1796 he met * Mary Wollstonecraft. Born in 1759, this remarkable woman had
illustrated in her own adventures the results of

* Apparently not for the first time; he had previously met
her in 1791.

the application of ideal laws to human life and society as at present constituted. Thrown on her own resources at eighteen years of age, she had been companion to a lady at Bath, and had then set up a school at Newington Green, where she became intimately acquainted with Dr. Richard Price. Failing there, she then became governess in a private family in Ireland, and had at last, in 1788, settled down to a literary life in London. Here she worked like a slave, battling very heroically both with poverty and ill-health. Gradually she had found friends, and among them Fuseli and his wife. Here she was brought into contact with the Reformers as they called themselves, among them Tom Paine. When Burke's " Reflections " had set London on fire and answers to it and apologies for it were pouring from every press, among the voices hers was one, and it found expression in a " Letter to Burke "— a running shriek of a painfully hysterical ring against Burke's arguments. Of a very different order was the next work, the " Vindication of the Rights of Women "—but to that I shall recur. In the heated atmosphere in which she lived she began now to lose her head, and not long afterwards her heart; for she fell frantically in love with Fuseli, Mrs. Fuseli, not unnaturally perhaps, objecting. So in 1792 this hyena in petticoats, this philosophising serpent—for such, I grieve to say, were the terms in which Horace Walpole spoke of her—went off to Paris, which she found in all the throes of the crisis preceding the execution of the King, whose passage to the guillotine she witnessed. Here she met Gilbert Imlay, fell frantically in love with him, and became his wife in the eyes of heaven, as one of her friends piously observed—but, unhappily, not in the eyes of the world. Imlay, who appears to have been a selfish and good-for-nothing fellow, not long afterwards deserted her. So back she came to England, with her child, a girl who was twenty-two years afterwards to die by her own hand. Maddened by Imlay's treatment, Mary threw herself into the Thames from Putney Bridge, but was rescued. Gradually she became calmer and resumed her literary work. Imlay was gradually forgotten and Godwin slowly took his place in Mary's affections. Neither of them believed in marriage, and though Mary had, he had not the courage to defy the world, so after living together for seven months they condescended to stoop to the marriage ceremony. Less than a year after, Mary died leaving the daughter who links the name of Godwin with that of Shelley. Not long afterwards Godwin married again. Let us see how. Next door to him in the Polygon, near Camden Town, where he then had a house, a Mrs. Clairmont with a son and daughter came to live. This lady fell in love with her illustrious neighbour, but did not know how to approach him, as his life was a very secluded one, and he was not a very accessible man, even though a neighbour. But she found that it was his habit to sit out on the balcony; upon that she took to sitting out on her balcony, which adjoined his, where she would gaze at him, but the absorbed philosopher gazed not back. At last she took courage and spoke. "Is it possible that I behold the immortal Godwin ?" It was so, as we know, and before the year was out the immortal Godwin was her own, and quite legally, for this terrible woman would not trifle with the law. This second Mrs. Godwin mismanaged his affairs, squandered his money, involved him in ruinous speculations, quarrelled with her own children, with his children, with him, and with his friends, had a strident voice, we are told, in incessant activity, wore green spectacles, and was altogether, said Charles Lamb in summary, "a very disgusting woman." However, Godwin was a philosopher, and they managed to rub on together.

And now came the most important event in Godwin's life. On January 3, 1812, Godwin received a letter. It informed him that the writer had been accustomed to consider him a luminary too dazzling for the darkness that surrounded him, that he had ardently desired to share on the footing of intimacy that intellect which he had delighted to contemplate in its emanations, but that he had long regarded him as a name enrolled in the list of the honourable dead and had felt regret that the glory of his being had passed from this world of ours.

Considering then these feelings [it said], you will not be surprised at the inconceivable emotions with which I learned your existence and your dwelling. . . . I have but just entered on the scene of human operations, yet my feelings and my reasonings correspond with what yours were.

And it concludes by imploring him to employ humanely half an hour in letting the writer know whether any hope could be held out to him of a personal interview. The writer of this letter was Percy Bysshe Shelley. Shelley was then in his twentieth year. He had as yet produced nothing which has contributed to his fame, but was then engaged on the " Retrospect," and was about to begin " Queen Mab." Between January and October he continued to correspond with his idol, and at the beginning of October the master and pupil met. All that Bolingbroke had been to Pope, Godwin now became to Shelley. The philosophy of Godwin, indeed, stands in precisely the same relation to the poetry of Shelley as the philosophical writings of Bolingbroke stand to the " Essay on Man," and as the writings of Democritus and Epicurus stood to the poem of Lucretius. A great part of " Queen Mab " is little more than a versification of " Political Justice." " The Revolt of Islam " is penetrated with the same influence ; so is the " Prometheus Unbound "; it inspires the Fragment of " Charles the First " ; it suffuses the " Ode to Liberty." It was the mainspring of all his social and political philosophy.

One of his prose essays, the Fragment of " A System of Government by Juries," is the commencement of a commentary on Godwin's theory of the application of a juridical system to government.

Another, the Fragment of the " Essay on Christianity," was evidently designed to show that the chief value of Christian doctrines is that they anticipated many of the teachings of Godwin.

Godwin was highly gratified by the homage paid to him and to his teachings by his fervid disciple, but when that homage took the form of a practical application of those teachings he forgot his philosophy and became as angry as the most unphilosophic and commonplace person might be. It is not quite clear when Shelley first met Mary Godwin, but it is certain that on June 8, 1814, a thrilling voice was calling "Shelley" and a thrilling voice was answering "Mary," and that these were the thrilling voices of two who had, to employ Professor Dowden's phrase,* become inexpressibly dear to one another. I need hardly remind you that at this time Shelley was the husband of a young wife, with two children. But as he had learned, and nowhere so emphatically as from his master, that the marriage tie is mere degradation when love has ceased, as his for his wife had done, he had as little scruple about dissolving the old tie as he had about forming a new one. Accordingly by the end of July Mary and Shelley were on their way to the Continent. Godwin's rage knew no bounds; he pronounced Shelley's offence against virtue to be beyond forgiveness, and when two months afterwards the fugitives returned he refused to have any intercourse with his too faithful disciple except through an attorney. But it must not be supposed that this intercourse through an attorney

* "Life of Shelley."

with the offender against virtue had any reference
to the offence. It was simply because Shelley
was assisting the philosopher with moneylenders
and backing bills for him, and the philosopher
fully appreciated the little services of this kind
which the prospective heir to a baronetcy and some
eighty thousand pounds was able to do for him.
Well might poor Mary, when commenting in her
Journal on her father's conduct, break into the
exclamation, " Oh, Philosophy ! " And oh, Philosophy ! indeed it was, and the results of philosophy were not to end here. Another inmate of
Godwin's household, a young girl, a daughter of
Mrs. Godwin by her first husband, had also, like
her half-sister, drunk deep from the fountains of
the " Political Justice." Meeting Byron, Byron
had no difficulty in persuading her to follow in
her half-sister's footsteps, though he did not
think it necessary to persuade her to defy the
world, and a miserable surreptitious intrigue was
the result, till her shame could no longer be
concealed. In September 1816 Fanny Imlay,
Mary Wollstonecraft's natural daughter, hopelessly in love with Shelley, distracted by the
miseries of her wretched home, in which the
straits of poverty were aggravated by the strident
turbulence of that very disgusting woman in
green spectacles, terminated her troubles by
poisoning herself at Swansea. A month after,
Harriet Shelley drowned herself in the Serpentine.
Early in the following year Godwin's principles
came into collision with the law and were submitted to the practical test of sanity and sound

sense. Lord Eldon, in stating his reasons for deciding that Shelley's children were not to remain in the exclusive custody of their father, but were to be placed under the protection of the court, thus expressed himself:

This is a case in which, as the matter appears to me, the father's principles cannot be misunderstood; in which his conduct, which I cannot but consider as highly immoral, has been established in proof and established as the effect of these principles; conduct nevertheless which he represents to himself and others, not as conduct to be considered immoral, but to be recommended and observed in practice, and as worthy of approbation. I consider this therefore as a case in which a father has demonstrated that he must and does deem it to be a matter of duty which his principles impose upon him to recommend to those whose opinions and habits he may take upon himself to form, that conduct in some of the most important relations of life as moral and virtuous which the law calls upon me to consider as immoral and vicious—conduct which the law animadverts upon as inconsistent with the duties of persons in such relations of life and which it considers as injuriously affecting both the interests of such persons and those of the community.

Godwin soon became reconciled with Shelley and Mary. In December 1816, little more than a fortnight after the inquest had been held on Harriet, they were duly married, and the philosopher was highly pleased. And this reconciliation was the more acceptable to him as a year before Shelley had come to terms with his father, who had consented to pay his debts and to allow him a thousand a year. As it was one of the fundamental principles of Godwin's philosophy that he who *has* should give to him who has not, and that there should be community of goods between those who were capable of profiting from them, and as the disciple had already proved himself so loyal, he naturally thought that things would begin to look up in Skinner Street. But unfortunately Godwin had many rivals. Peacock wanted a hundred a year. Leigh Hunt wanted all he could get. Charles Clairmont had formed a scheme to live a Wordsworthian life among the Pyrenees—plus, I regret to say, a Miss Jeanne Morel—and " Do I dream, my dear Shelley," writes this youth, " when a gleam of gay hope gives me reason to doubt of the *impossibility* of my scheme ? " But loud above all these voices, which were after all pleading soft and low for luxuries, rose the piercing cry, and it was always rising, from Skinner Street :

" Five hundred pounds ! . . . a struggle sometimes almost beyond human strength." " Once every three months," he wrote to Shelley, " do I throw myself beneath the feet of Taylor of Norwich and my other discounting friends, protesting that this is absolutely for the last time. Shall this ever have an end ? " *

Godwin certainly worked hard, but he imposed unmercifully upon Shelley, and not on Shelley alone, but on any one he could get at.

Shelley will meet us no more, but who can take leave of his early associations, his informing surroundings, without calling to mind Matthew Arnold's commentary ?

What a set, what a world ! is the exclamation that breaks from us as we come to the end of this history of " the occurrences

---

* Dowden's " Life of Shelley."

of Shelley's private life." . . . Godwin's house of sordid horror and Godwin preaching and holding the hat, and the green-spectacled Mrs. Godwin, and Hogg the faithful friend—

you will remember that he had attempted to induce Harriet to leave Shelley—

and Hunt the Horace of this precious world . . . and Lord Byron with his deep grain of coarseness and commonness, his affectation, his brutal selfishness—what a set ! *

What a set, we may add, for that Bird of Paradise to have got his radiant wings entangled with !

And now to pass to Godwin's work, " The Enquiry concerning Political Justice and its Influence on Morals and Happiness." I may mention in passing that I shall deal, not with the first edition, in quarto, which appeared in 1793, and which contained much that was altered and very much that was modified afterwards, but with the second edition, in octavo, which appeared in 1796, and may be regarded as Godwin's final gospel. By Political Justice he means, he tells us, the adoption of any principle of morality and truth into the practice of a community, and the inquiry instituted was therefore an inquiry into the principles of society, of government, and of morals. The first part deals with principles, the second with the mode in which those principles should be applied in politics and in society. The general purport of the work is indicated in the fourth book :

* " Essays in Criticism."

The adherents of the old systems of government affirm, " that the imbecility of the human mind is such as to make it unadvisable that man should be trusted with himself : that his genuine condition is that of perpetual pupillage : that he is regulated by passions and partial views and cannot be governed by pure reason and undiluted truth : that it is the business of a wise man not to subvert either in himself or in others delusions which are useful and prejudices which are salutary : and that he is the worst enemy of his species who attempts in whatever mode to introduce a form of society where no advantage is taken to restrain us from vices by illusion from which we cannot be restrained by reason." . . . Tenets the opposite of these constitute the great outline of the present work.

As I am not dealing with this book in detail, a succinct review of some of its leading doctrines must suffice. Locke has observed that the difference between the reasoning of a fool and of a madman is that a fool reasons incorrectly on just data and that a madman reasons correctly on absurd data. No one can accuse Godwin of any inconsistency in his reasoning, of any flaw in his logical process. Grant his hypotheses and his conclusions follow as necessarily as the conclusion follows the premise in the syllogism, follows as certainly as the arithmetical fact that two and two make four. But his hypotheses involve, not merely the demolition and reconstruction of the whole fabric of society and government, but of human nature itself. His leading assumptions are the perfectibility of man and the omnipotence of reason. He contends that that noble animal man, so far from being what religion and law had assumed him to be, a fallen creature saturated with original sin and desperately wicked; so far from being what every political community in the world had assumed him to be, a thing to be coerced and restrained—a very devil in a strait jacket—was by instinct and nature precisely the opposite of all this. Leave him to himself and his will would secrete virtue as naturally as his liver secretes bile; remove the restrictions and impediments which have been placed in the way of his upward aspiring instincts and impulses, his natural benevolence, humanity, and unselfishness, and the millennium would be realised. Reason is omnipotent: it should be the sole motive of action, the sole guide of action; the sole criterion of truth and virtue: all other motives, guides, and criteria are illusions. Man being, as he naturally is, a virtuous and reasonable creature, an appeal to his reason not only ought to be the only form which coercion should assume, but it would be an appeal which would be infallibly successful. Two other fundamental propositions are the natural equality of rights consequent on natural equality at birth, and the idea of the General Good as the supreme tribunal at which everything is to be tried.

Now it is not difficult to see how every human institution and system, political, moral, and religious, is likely to fare when cast into this metaphysical crucible. Society is reduced to an aggregate of independent individuals with no respect for tradition, with no prescriptive rights and privileges, bound by no pacts. Each his own legislator, each free and indeed bound to act just as his particular measure of reason directs:

hereditary titles become mere gewgaws: hereditary property dissolves into—to employ Godwin's words—"a mouldy patent shewn as a right to extort from neighbours what the labour of those neighbours has produced." Every form of coercive government becomes immoral and iniquitous: any form of government an evil—"a usurpation," as he puts it, "upon the private judgment and individual conscience of mankind ": religious establishments mere insults to human intelligence, designed to perpetuate a system of blind submission and abject hypocrisy. Morality dissolves itself into the correct calculation of consequences, the beneficial or pernicious tendency of any action alone constituting it virtuous or vicious. No institution or system indeed survives the test of Godwin's remorseless analysis. But to his condemnation of one institution a particular interest is attached:

The institution of marriage is a system of fraud, and men who carefully mislead their judgments in the daily affair of their life must always have a crippled judgment in every other concern. We ought to dismiss our mistake as soon as it is detected, but we are taught to cherish it. . . . Marriage, as now understood, is a monopoly, and the worst of monopolies. So long as two human beings are forbidden by positive institution to follow the dictates of their own mind, prejudice will ever be alive and vigorous. So long as I seek by despotic and artificial means to engross a woman to myself and to prohibit any neighbour from proving his superior claim, I am guilty of the most odious selfishness. Over this imaginary prize men watch with perpetual jealousy; and one finds his desire and his capacity to circumvent as much excited as the other is excited to traverse his projects and frustrate his hopes. As long as this state of society continues, philanthropy will be crossed and checked in a thousand ways, and the still augmenting stream of abuse will continue to flow. The abolition of marriage in the form now practised will be attended with no evils.*

He then goes on coolly to discuss whether a universal system of free love would be preferable to a system in which a " man will select for himself a partner to whom he will adhere as long as that adherence shall continue to be the choice of both parties." He is inclined on the whole to think the latter course would be most conducive to the public good. The imperturbable serenity with which Godwin lays down his monstrous hypotheses and pursues them to their equally monstrous conclusions is perhaps the most extraordinary feature of his work. This is partly to be attributed to his own abnormal temperament and partly perhaps to the utter absence in him of any sense of humour, if it had not a more *vulgar* origin, mere indulgence in paradoxical vanity. He was himself a person of frigid temper and signally deficient on the side of the emotions, without what Coleridge calls " the illumination of the heart." It never seems to have occurred to him that man cannot by any process be transformed into a logical mill for grinding out philanthropical virtues, and that, even if he could, the result would only be the petrification of life. Let us examine for a moment the unit of Godwin's ideal state. He would be without passion, without emotion, without sentiment. His God would be the public good, and every act of his life would be a sacrifice to that idol. To that he would refer everything.

* Bk. VIII. 8.

If he had the alternative of saving a mother, a wife, a father, a child, or a perfect stranger from death, and he were satisfied that the life of the stranger was of more importance to mankind, he would save the stranger and leave those who were bound to him by mere claims of affection to perish. He would form or dissolve ties on a similar principle. He would make love for the public good, or for the public good he would remain celibate. He would be Scævola and Curtius, Brutus and Cato in quintessence. He would neither feel gratitude nor expect it, knowing that what he received he received merely as the proper recipient, and what he gave he gave for the same reason. He would not raise a glass of wine to his lips or annex an ornament to his person without satisfying himself that their production had involved no unjust condition of labour. Personal sympathies or personal antipathies he would have none. He would be one whom no intimacy could endear, no kindness attach, no injuries provoke, no beauty charm. Such is Godwin's ideal unit, and would you have the picture of the millennium which the aggregation of these units will realise, here it is in his own words :

The men, therefore, whom we are supposing to exist when the earth shall refuse itself to a more extended population, will probably cease to propagate. They will no longer have any motive, either of error or reason, to induce them. The whole will be a people of men, and not of children. Generation will not succeed generation, nor truth have in a certain degree to recommence her career at the end of every thirty years. There will be no war, no crimes, no administration of justice as it is called, and no government. Beside this, there will be no disease, no anguish, no melancholy, and no resentment. Every man will seek with ineffable ardour the good of all. Mind will be active and eager, yet never disappointed. Men will see the progressive advancement of virtue and good and feel that if things occasionally happen contrary to their hopes, the miscarriage itself was a necessary part of that progress. They will know that they are members of the chain, that each has his several utility, and they will not feel indifferent to that utility. They will be eager to enquire into the good that already exists, the means by which it was produced and the greater good that is yet in store. They will never want motives for exertion; for that benefit which a man thoroughly understands and earnestly loves, he cannot refrain from endeavouring to promote.*

We contemplate Godwin's Utopia with its ideal unit and its polity of ideal units with something of the feeling with which Macbeth contemplated the spectre of Banquo. It cannot indeed be said that this frigid phantasma of the pure reason, this stark and pallid mockery of life, has no " speculation " in the eyes with which it glares on the inquirer; but for the rest it is certainly all Banquo: " Avaunt!" [we cry] . . . " thy bones are marrowless, thy blood is cold."†

Godwin's ruthless reduction of all that gives life its grace, its colour, its charm, nay, its real meaning, into the *caput mortuum* of mere reason is not only in the highest degree repulsive, but absurd and ridiculous. Hobbes and Swift had attempted to do the same thing before him, and if the " Leviathan " had succeeded the

* Bk. VIII. 9.   † "Macbeth," iii. 4.

Revolution and the creator of the King of
Brobdingnag had, under the same impulse, tried
his hand at a Utopia, Literature might have
witnessed the singular spectacle of the extremes
of cynicism passing by precisely the same process
into the extremes of optimism. Godwin never
seems to have reflected that pure reason in its
application to conduct and life is a very insufficient
and treacherous guide; it conducted *him* to the
perfectibility of man and to the millennium: it
conducted Falstaff to the rejection of honour.
Remove all that Godwin removed—transcendental and sentimental considerations—and how
unanswerable is Falstaff's logic with the un-
answerableness of Godwin's own:

Honour pricks me on.   Yea, but how if honour prick me off
when I come on ?—How then ?   Can honour set a leg ?   No.
Or an arm ?   No.   Or take away the grief of a wound ?   No.—
Honour hath no skill in surgery then ?   No.   What is Honour ?
A word.   What is *in* that word honour ?   What *is* that honour ?
Air.   A trim reckoning !—Who hath it ?   He that died o'
Wednesday.   Doth he feel it ?   No.   Doth he hear it ?   No.
Is it insensible then ?   Yea, to the dead.   But will it not live
with the living ?   No.   Why ?   Detraction will not suffer it;
therefore I'll none of it.   Honour is a mere scutcheon: and so
ends my catechism.*

Well might Troilus say:

> Nay, if we talk of reason
> Let's shut our gates and sleep.   Manhood and Honour
> Should have hare hearts would they but fat their thoughts
> With this crammed reason.†

---

* "King Henry IV." (Part I.), v. 1.
† "Troilus and Cressida," ii. 2.

But it would be doing Godwin great injustice not to acknowledge that there is much in his work which is of real value. It is well that the institutions which he arraigns should be submitted to such tests as he applies to them, not as a test of their title to existence, but as a test of their applicability to modification. It is well that the questions which he discusses should be approached on the side on which he approaches them lest one good custom should corrupt the world. Many of his remarks on aristocracy, on the restrictions laid upon the virtuous energies of man, on free will and necessity, on revolutions, on good and evil, are excellent. And his note is sometimes really noble, as read his reply to those who would not assist in negro emancipation on the ground that the slaves are contented :

It is not very material to a man of liberal and enlarged mind whether they are contented or no. Are they contented ? I am not contented for them. I see in them beings of certain capacities equal to certain pursuits and enjoyments. It is of no consequence in the question that they do not see this, that they do not know their interests and happiness. They do not repine ? Neither does a stone repine. That which you mention as an alleviation finishes in my conception the portrait of their calamity. Abridged as they are of independence and enjoyment, they have neither the apprehension nor the spirit of men. I cannot bear to see human nature thus degraded. It is my duty, if I can, to make themselves a thousand times happier than they are. [*]

Again, in the same chapter:

The man who has sought to benefit nations rises above the mechanical ideas of barter and exchange. He asks no gratitude.

---

[*] Bk. IV. 11.

To see that they are benefited, or to believe that they will be so, is its own reward. He ascends to the highest of human pleasures, the pleasures of disinterestedness. He enjoys all the good that mankind possesses, and all the good that he perceives to be in reserve for them. No man so truly promotes his own interest as he that forgets it. No man reaps so copious a harvest of pleasure as he who thinks only of the pleasure of other men.

It must be admitted that nothing lends itself so easily to eloquence which finds a response in every liberal mind as the themes of the " Political Justice," and that passages like these, and they are many, do not compensate the radical unsoundness and pernicious tendency of this most extravagant work, a work of which it may be said, as was said with less truth of another, that a foolish man could not have written it and that a wise man would not.

But to turn from Godwin to Mary Wollstonecraft and her work. I have already given a sketch of her life and shown how the Revolution affected her, and how she wrote her foolish and intemperate " Letter to Burke." This subject was followed up four years later by the first volume of " An Historical and Modern View of the French Revolution." Neither of these works is of any interest now, and therefore I shall say no more about them, merely remarking that the second is of a very different character from the first, being comparatively sane and sober. But the work by which she is remembered and which deserves to be remembered is the work which we will now consider.

On July 3, 1790, she drew up a petition pleading

for the admission of women to the right of citizenship, and on July 12, at an assembly in the Palais Royal, the Abbé Fauchet, accompanied by a Dutch lady, Madame Palm Aedler, addressed the assembly in an eloquent speech on that subject. For some months women had not only been present at the meetings of the Jacobins in the Rue St. Honoré, but had taken part in the debates, and Madame Palm Aedler, supported by Condorcet and Fauchet, now determined to press for their right to engage in public affairs, not as mere interlopers and accidents, but as having authority. But the movement was not successful. In a pamphlet published by Talleyrand, who was not in favour of the admission of women to these rights, he had conceded " that to see one half of the human race excluded by the other from all participation of government was a political phenomenon that according to abstract principles it was impossible to explain." On that hint Mary Wollstonecraft spoke, and she dedicated her " Vindication of the Rights of Women " to Talleyrand, whom she had met in London in 1792, just before the book was published. It was to induce Talleyrand to support the movement in France, where the question was the political equality of the sexes, hoping no doubt that it would form a precedent and extend to England. This plea is included in her vindication, but no stress is laid on it, the stress being laid only on educational equality.

The purport of her work she describes in summary herself :

Contending for the rights of woman, my main argument is built on this simple principle, that if she be not prepared by education to become the companion of man, she will stop the progress of knowledge and virtue ; for truth must be common to all or it will be inefficacious with respect to its influence on general practice. And how can woman be expected to co-operate unless she know why she ought to be virtuous ? unless freedom strengthen her reason till she comprehend her duty and see in what manner it is connected with her real good ? If children are to be educated to understand the true principle of patriotism, their mother must be a patriot, and the love of mankind from which an orderly train of virtues spring can only be produced by considering the moral and civil interest of mankind : but the education and situation of woman at present shuts her out from such investigations.*

She then proceeds to say that she shall consider women " in the grand light of human creatures who in common with men are placed on this Earth to unfold their faculties," † and that her exhortation will not be addressed to " ladies " only, to whom such serious instruction as has hitherto been conferred on woman has been practically confined, but more particularly to those of the middle class. She then reviews the prevalent theories about the education proper for women, giving especial prominence to Rousseau, who in his " Émile " had contended that women were constitutionally unfitted for studies which tend to generalise ideas, such as the exact sciences; that works of genius are beyond their capacity ; that their sphere is the heart, not the head, their spring impulse, not reason, and that their chief study should be man, to understand him

* Dedication to Talleyrand.   † Introduction.

and to please and fascinate him; that they are
essentially unreasoning creatures, but the more
charming and delightful because of that.
The other writers whom she reprobates are
Milton, but more especially Dr. Gregory, Dr.
Fordyce, and Mrs. Barbauld, who were then
great authorities on women's education. They
had inculcated just the conventional notions
about woman and her relation to man and to the
scheme of life, which may be said to be summed
up in the pretty lines which Dryden puts into
the mouth of Raphael when addressing Adam
about Eve:

> Thy stronger soul shall her weak Reason sway,
> And then, through love, her beauty shall obey:
> Thou shalt secure her helpless sex from harms,
> And she thy cares shall sweeten with her charms.*

All this, she contends, had tended to degrade
women, to place them in a most false and
unworthy position, and all this she illustrates
comprehensively by citing a copy of verses by
Mrs. Barbauld, indignantly emphasising portions
by italics:

> Flowers to the fair: to you these flowers I bring
> And strive to greet you with an earlier Spring.
> *Flowers sweet and gay and delicate like you;*
> *Emblems of innocence, and beauty too.*
>
> *   *   *   *   *   *
>
> *Flowers the sole luxury which Nature knew*
> In Eden's pure and guileless garden grew.

---

* "State of Innocence," Act ii. sc. 1.

To loftier forms are rougher tasks assign'd ;
The sheltering oak resists the stormy wind,
The tougher yew repels invading foes,
And the tall pine for future navies grows ;
But this soft family, to cares unknown,
Were born for pleasure and delight alone.
Gay without toil and lovely without art,
They spring to cheer the sense and glad the heart.
Nor blush, my fair, to own you copy these ;
Your *best*, your sweetest empire is—to please.*

Now till women come to understand that this sort of thing is the grossest insult that can be offered them, the kind of homage which they ought indignantly to repudiate, there will be small hope of their becoming what God and Nature had fitted them to become. It was no doubt very gratifying to the tyrant man to find that he had a monopoly in all that makes life important and honourable, very gratifying to be looked up to as a demi-god and to have these lovely creatures, these " emblems of innocence and beauty too," clinging helplessly to him for support, he supporting them just as long as it happened to be agreeable to him to support them, and then when the parasite ceased to be lovely or attractive letting it drop and collapse in ruin or how it might. She complains that the whole education of women tends in this direction to make them " fine by defect and amiably weak," to make them believe seriously that their end and aim had been summed up in Lord Lyttelton's precept :

* " To a Lady with some Painted Flowers."

One only care your gentle breasts should move,
Th' important business of your life is love.*

Wholly erroneous notions of what constitutes
modesty, decorum, and propriety, tending rather
to the corruption of woman than to her enlighten-
ment, cry aloud for reformation. She is very
severe on the weak superstitions, the sentimentalism, the over-attention to dress, the
ignorance of all that concerns the rearing and
educating of children, then prevalent among
women—all of which she attributes to absurdly
mistaken notions as to the discipline proper for
them. Her remarks on education are very
sensible, and in her scheme for combining what
was best in public and what was best in private
education, contending that it should be under-
taken by Government, she anticipated what is
with some modification our present national
school system, just as in her scheme for the
education of young children she anticipated the
Froebel system. In a word, she would have
training directed to fitting a woman for the
severe duties of life—let their constitution be
braced by athletics and such pursuits as gardening,
their minds by the study of experimental philosophy and serious literature, their character
by free intercourse with the world. Let such
professions be opened to them as they are fitted
to fill, especially medicine, surgery, and the care
of the sick. All this is expressed, it must be
owned, in a style which is too often exceedingly

* " Advice to a Lady."

slipshod and too often offensively bombastic, and, what is worse, with touches of coarseness which plainly indicate that, in acquiring the virtues of man, woman is in some danger of acquiring them at a heavy loss. Like most reactionists she goes too far. She under-estimates, and that contemptuously, *all* that constitutes the *charm* of woman. In making "reason" the criterion and standard of everything she lays herself open to refutation by Nature herself. But on the whole it may be pronounced to be an admirable work—temperate, reasonable, and eloquent with the eloquence of really rational enthusiasm. It certainly marked and contributed to initiate a new era in the history of woman; it gave a great impulse to that movement which has been one of the most striking and important movements of the present age—the higher education of women and the vindication of woman's right to share and assist in all those aspirations, aims, and achievements which constitute the dignity of human nature and are the glory of the human race. One of the rights for which she pleaded still remains unattained—more than one half of every political community is still excluded from all participation in its government—woman has not yet the suffrage. But patience, ladies, your time is coming and is probably now hard at hand, but whether for good or whether for the opposite that same time alone can tell.

To the two writers whom we have been considering great and permanent interest attaches itself quite apart from any question of the intrinsic value of their works, for the teachings of the one, humanised, beautified, consecrated, have been embodied in poetry which is among the glories of our language and can only perish with the language; and to the other belongs the honour of sounding the trumpet for the most important social revolution of modern times.

WORDSWORTH AS A TEACHER

MAN in action and in relation to action and time is the theme of Shakespeare; man in spirit and in relation to spirit and the eternal is the theme of Wordsworth. The least transcendental of poets is Shakespeare; of all poets the most purely transcendental is Wordsworth. Shakespeare, in a phrase which was applied to Aristotle, is the " secretary of Nature who dipped his pen in mind ": this and much else, but this primarily. He is pre-eminently the poet of this world, *spectator ac particeps,* in relation to its doings and struggles. *Above* it by virtue of the comprehensiveness and completeness of his vision, by virtue of his seeing life steadily and seeing it whole. But the highest conclusion to which he has given direct voice finds its expression in humorous irony on the one side, and in majestic threnody on the other. " Lord, what fools these mortals be ! " is the note of the first; and the note of the second is:

> The cloud-capped towers, the gorgeous palaces,
> The solemn temples, the great globe itself,
> Yea, all which it inherit, shall dissolve ;
> And, like this insubstantial pageant faded,
> Leave not a rack behind : We are such stuff

As dreams are made of, and our little life
Is rounded with a sleep.*

And, like Nature in Tennyson's personification, "he knows no more." We feel that, could we have questioned him, as to the fate of what Death dissolves, and asked him in his inspiration, "*Can* these *live ?*" the answer would have been the answer of the Hebrew prophet: "O Lord God, *Thou* knowest."

But where Shakespeare is silent, there Wordsworth speaks. A rapt enthusiast, a contemplative philosopher and seer, living by admiration, hope and love, "breathing in worlds to which the Heaven of Heavens is but a veil"; not with Erato or Clio, but with Urania as his guide, he aspires to enter and unlock that world—the world of Form, of Essence, of Ideas. Of all poets the most spiritual and transcendental, with him the celestial and the terrestrial are so essentially blended that the latter *is*, only in so far as it reflects the former, related as intimately as shadow is related to substance. All great poets are divine, but to Wordsworth is the title preeminently applicable. In relation to the τὸ θεῖον, to divinity does he read life, does he interpret life, does he speculate on life—the life of the past, of the present, of the future. Let us think of Shakespeare and Wordsworth together—of Shakespeare as the poet of man and of the world-drama ; of Wordsworth as the poet of Nature, of the world, of essence and spirit. A time will

* "Tempest," iv. I.

come, indeed it will, when to many thousands
those two names will stand at the head of English
poetry. Matthew Arnold has already given him
the first place among English poets after Shakespeare and Milton, for reasons which do not take
into consideration some of the highest qualities of
his poetry. It is difficult to understand Matthew
Arnold's silence about the significance of Wordsworth's metaphysical philosophy; and his prophetic insight gives him that place simply because
of the extraordinary power with which he feels
the joy offered to us in Nature, the joy offered to
us in the simple, primary affections and duties,
and because of the extraordinary power with
which in case after case he shows us this joy and
renders it so as to make us share it; gives him
this place mainly on the strength of the unique
power found in such poems as " Michael," " The
Fountain " and " The Solitary Reaper." What
will become more and more detractive from
Milton's influence as time goes on and the world
sweeps more and more into the broader day will
be the hideous and revolting anthropomorphism
of much of his theology—an anthropomorphism
not like that of the Greeks, sanely, soundly, nobly
symbolic, but *often* and more than *accidentally*
un-sane, unsound, not noble. In the serene region
in which the genius of Wordsworth dwelt, how
often, how habitually he

> Came on that which *is* and caught
> The deep pulsations of the world.*

* Tennyson's " In Memoriam," xcv. 39.

To him, rather than to Shakespeare, may we say that "the prophetic spirit" spoke articulate things. No vision of future Utopia, none of those visions which even now we have seen realised, seem to have been unfolded to Shakespeare. He appears to have no conception of the immense future of the people, of times when the individual within and the world is more and more, of the new majesties of mighty states, of the power and the triumphs of enthusiasm in things spiritual as in things temporal—of what, in a word, has been wrought since 1790, of what is now in course of certain evolution, not a whisper of all this. If this is to be explained historically, so be it ; but it is a fact. But the future will find in Wordsworth its foreseer and its prophet.

> Paradise, and groves
> Elysian, Fortunate Fields—like those of old
> Sought in the Atlantic Main—why should they be
> A history only of departed things,
> Or a mere fiction of what never was ?
> For the discerning intellect of Man,
> When wedded to this goodly Universe
> In love and holy passion, shall find these
> A simple produce of the common day.
> I, long before the blissful hour arrives,
> Would chant, in lonely peace, the spousal verse
> Of this great consummation :
>
> .   .   .   .
>
> Descend, prophetic Spirit ! that inspir'st
> The human Soul of universal earth,
> Dreaming on things to come.*

* From the first book of " The Recluse." *See* preface to " The Excursion."

· No, we have not done justice to Wordsworth, and we have not done him justice because we have not taken him seriously enough. We have treated his great poem—all his poetry is one great poem—just as we generally treat God's great poem, the world, yielding ourselves to its sensuous charms, busying ourselves with its accidents and phenomena ; enjoying a landscape here, a pretty dell there, a picturesque object, a delicate blossom, a stately tree : chipping rocks about, plucking flowers and delighting ourselves with the perfume in them, in the case of the one ; in the case of the other, culling out a fine passage, a graceful sonnet or lyric, a felicitous expression, a dainty touch. And this it is quite right that we should do : the first object of poetry is to give pleasure. The chattering schoolmaster abroad in Nature and among poets is apt to be an annoying superfluity. But let us remember this—and if the schoolmaster reminds us of it, let us be very grateful—that the measure of our enjoyment of these things is proportioned to our power of really understanding, is proportioned to our serious striving to get true insight into them. Let us try to read God's poem in the spirit of Tennyson's lines :

> Flower in the crannied wall,
> I pluck you out of the crannies ;
> I hold you here, root and all, in my hand,
> Little flower—but *if* I could understand
> What you are, root and all and all in all,
> I should know what God and Man is.*

---

* " Flower in the Crannied Wall."

And in like manner we should in reading Wordsworth's great poem try to penetrate his full
meaning, to *feel* his full meaning, say, in such
passages as these :

> To me the meanest flower that blows can give
> Thoughts that do often lie too deep for tears ; *

or

> All things, responsive to the writing, there
> Breathed immortality, revolving life,
> And greatness still revolving ; infinite :
> There littleness was not ; the least of things
> Seemed infinite.†

Truly may we apply to Wordsworth his own
lines :

> A mind
> That feeds upon infinity, that broods
> Over the dark abyss, intent to hear
> Its voices issuing forth to silent light
> In one continuous stream ; a mind sustain'd
> By recognitions of transcendent power,
> In sense conducting to ideal form,
> In soul of more than mortal privilege.‡

" To console the afflicted : to add sunshine to
daylight by making the happy happier : to teach
the young and the gracious of every age to see,
to think and feel ; and therefore to become more
actively and securely virtuous—this is their office
(he is referring to his poems), which I trust they
will faithfully perform long after we (that is,

* "Ode to Immortality."   † "Excursion," i. 227.
          ‡ "The Prelude," xiv. 70.

all that is mortal of us) are mouldered in our graves." *

This, then, was what he aimed at and what he aspired to do.

We are to look on all Wordsworth's poems as forming parts of one vast design, having a great central purpose—it was to deal with man and the world, on man, on Nature and in human life—of truth, of grandeur, beauty, love and hope. And melancholy fear subdued by faith

Of blessed consolations in distress :
Of moral strength, and intellectual Power ;
Of joy in widest commonalty spread :
Of the individual Mind that keeps her own
Inviolate retirement, subject there
To Conscience only, and the law supreme
Of that Intelligence which governs all—†

—the mind of man is to be the haunt and main region of his song : he should " descend on earth or dwell in highest heaven," and

breathe in worlds
To which the heaven of heavens is but a veil.‡

But if so mighty a work was to be accomplished, the first thing to be ascertained was whether he was equal to the task. He must first know himself—he must take a review of his own mind and examine how far Nature and education had qualified him for this employment ; and so he proceeded to write his autobiography, recording

* Letter to Lady Beaumont, May 21, 1807.
† From the first book of " The Recluse."
‡ Ibid.

his experiences, positive, metaphysical and moral.
And this self-anatomy is embodied in the " Prelude," fourteen books begun in 1799 and completed in 1805. This preliminary work, which was
to have stood in the same relation to the work
following it as the ante-chamber to the body of
a Gothic church, having been finished, was to
have been followed by " The Recluse." This
poem was to have been completed in three parts.
Of the *first* part only the first book was completed,
and that remained in MS.—fragments only
having been published—till 1888. The second
part is represented by the " Excursion," in nine
books ; and the " Excursion " forms a part
of the dramatic portion of the design—that
is to say, characters are introduced recording
their experiences, sentiments and reflections ;
in the other portions of the work the poet only
speaks.

Now, no serious student of Wordsworth will
hold these poems lightly—they contain some of
his most precious teaching. But we all feel that
they are a *failure*, that on the whole they are
bald, prosy and dull : the thoughts are often
flat and commonplace, and inordinately spun out :
the style is often harsh and jejune, often on the
other hand turgid and verbose. Homer sometimes nods, but Wordsworth snores ; and he is
capable of snoring on for three or four hundred
lines—there is one stretch of seven hundred. Go
to the " Prelude " and " Excursion," O younger
student of Wordsworth, only when you have
become initiated. Wordsworth probably felt

himself that this enormous philosophical poem was, and would be, a veritable failure, and appears himself to have got weary of it. But now let us turn to the part of the great design which was *not* a failure. In his preliminary account of the design, after comparing the " Prelude " in its relation to the " Recluse " to the ante-chamber of a Gothic cathedral, he had said, " continuing this allusion, he (the author) may be permitted to add that his Minor Pieces . . . when they shall be properly arranged, will be found by the attentive reader to have such connection with the main Work as may give them claim to be likened to the little cells, oratories and sepulchral recesses ordinarily included in those edifices." We shall do well to remember this ; we need not press it too closely, for, of course, Wordsworth composed fragmentarily as the mood and the incident inspired, and we need not let any continuous attention to the relation in which particular poems stand to the whole to interfere with our enjoyment. But for all that, it is well to remember, just as it is very easy to see, that all his poems are parts of one great whole. Nature and man, then, are his themes. We have learnt to associate him so entirely with Nature, as Nature is generally understood, that it is well for us to bear in mind that his poems exhibit man in his *essentially* human character and relations as child, as parent, as husband, *i.e.* the *qualities* which are common to all men as opposed to those which distinguish one man from another.   This is undoubtedly one great and important feature in his work, a feature which is easily overlooked and worthy, therefore, of all the emphasis with which Wordsworth has directed attention to it. But this is very far from being its predominant feature. This will account for the attractiveness of much of his work, just as his faculty of catching and rendering so wonderfully the power and charm of Nature will account also for another part of that attractiveness. But we know, just as he knew, that nine-tenths of his readers would not know that that was not his grand mission. In the preface to the " Lyrical Ballads " he said in effect of the poet that he is an inspired philosopher, the interpreter of Nature and of human life to the uninitiated ; that it is his function to discover spiritual and moral significance in objects and incidents where the common eye sees neither the one nor the other. In his own magnificent phrase, true poets are " lords of the visionary eye," and the work of the poet in its most exalted activity is to pierce through the obscuring veil of mere phenomena to essence, spirit to spirit, soul to soul. So over and over again has he thanked God for having given him the power to free himself, if only at rare intervals, from the shackles of sensuous existence and catch glimpses of the world of being.

There are two powers in the world about which a word or two may be appropriately said by way of prelude to Wordsworth's philosophy : the one is *Platonism*, the other is *Stoicism*. Of Wordsworth's relation to Platonism the point to note is that it was conscious. Wordsworth had

read Plato, the " Phædo " certainly, and had
adopted as much of the doctrine of the ideal—
I put it comprehensively—as seemed to him
compatible with truth. But the interest of his
relation to Stoicism is much greater, for there do
not appear to be any traces of his having paid
any attention to it : I can find no indication in
his Biography that he had read a word of Seneca
or Epictetus, or Marcus Aurelius. It would not
be too much to say that the germ of very many
of the leading and distinguishing philosophical
tenets of Wordsworth, ethical and metaphysical
alike, will be found in the writings of the Stoical
school ; and where he is not Stoical he is Platonic.

Let us take first one of his leading characteristics—his *Pantheism*. Wordsworth is a Pantheist in one sense, and is not a Pantheist in
another—this will be explained presently. The
Pantheism of the Stoics may be thus summed up :
The universe is one great animal, pervaded by
one soul or presence of life. Into man as a fraction
of the whole, as a limb of this body, is transfused
a portion of the universal spirit. The individual
soul bears the same relation to the soul of the
universe that a part does to the whole. At the
end of the world's course the individual soul will
be resolved into the primary substance, into the
Divine Being. God is the soul, the mind, the
reason of the world, as being a united whole
containing in Himself the germ of all things.
The world is the sum of all real existence, and
all real existence is originally contained in God,
who is at once universal matter and the creative

force which fashions matter into the particular elements. In point of being, God and the world are the same. The two points, it will be seen, in which this differs from Wordsworth is, first, in its gross materialism, and in the absence of any distinction between the existence of God and external nature. In all other respects the poet and the philosopher are at one. But what a divine enthusiasm animates the poet! This is an important point, and let me give one or two illustrations:

> To every Form of being is assign'd
> An *active* Principle; howe'er remov'd
> From sense and observation, it subsists
> In all things, in all natures; in the stars
> Of azure heaven, the unenduring clouds,
> In flower and tree, in every pebbly stone
> That paves the brooks, the stationary rocks,
> The moving waters, and the invisible air.
>
> Spirit that knows no insulated spot,
> No chasm, no solitude, from link to link
> It circulates, the Soul of all the worlds.*

Again, in " Tintern Abbey ":

> I have felt
> A presence that disturbs me with the joy
> Of elevated thoughts; a sense sublime
> Of something far more deeply interfused,
> Whose dwelling is the light of setting suns,
> And the round Ocean and the living air,
> And the blue sky, and in the mind of man:
> A motion and a spirit, that impels
> All thinking things, all objects of all thought,
> And rolls through all things.

---

* " Excursion," ix. 1.

And so again in the " Lines written in Early Spring " :

> To her fair works did Nature link
> The human soul that through me ran ;

Everything is alike ; through all runs the same soul :

> And 'tis my faith that every flower
> Enjoys the air it breathes.*

So in the poem entitled " Nutting," where he tells how

> the shady nook
> Of hazels, and the green and mossy bower,
> Deform'd and sullied, patiently gave up
> Their quiet being :
>
> .   .   .   .   .
>
> Then, dearest maiden, move along these shades
> In gentleness of heart : with gentle hand
> Touch—for there is a spirit in the woods.

So we can understand his mystic love of bird and flower, the significance of Nature's meanest and humblest objects. We can understand the meaning of those lines in the "Old Cumberland Beggar " :

> 'Tis Nature's law
> That none, the meanest of created things
> Or forms created the most vile and brute,
> The dullest or most noxious, should exist
> Divorc'd from good, a spirit and pulse of good
> A life and soul, to every mode of being
> Inseparably link'd.

And now we come to the second great point

* " Lines written in Early Spring."

of Stoicism in connection with Wordsworth—
the living according to Nature.   This was the
virtue of Stoicism, the ζῆν κατὰ φύσιν—this was
to bring man's action into harmony with the
rest of the universe and with the general order
of the world.   And it was a virtue which implied
two things.   On the one hand, the resignation of
the individual to the universe, obedience to the
universal law ;   on the other hand, it involves the
harmony of man with himself—the dominion of
his higher over his lower nature, of reason over
passion, and the rising superior to everything
which does not belong to his true nature.   So too
when Chrysippus tells us that all ethical enquiries
must start with considering the universal order
and arrangement of the world, and that it is only
by a study of Nature and of what God is that anything really satisfactory can be stated about good
and evil, we see how near we are to Wordsworth :
it is exactly

> One impulse from a vernal wood
>   May teach you more of man,
> Of moral evil and of good,
>   Than all the sages can.*

To Wordsworth the Stoic would present himself as

> One to whose smooth-rubbed soul can cling
> Nor form, nor feeling, great or small ;
> A reasoning, self-sufficing thing,
> An intellectual All in all ! †

---

* " The Tables Turned."   † " A Poet's Epitaph."

And perhaps in that verse he had the Stoic in his mind.

Of course in many essential points Wordsworth differs from the tenets and ideals of Stoicism. Nothing, for example, could be further removed from it than his inculcation of humility, his insistence on man's walking by admiration, love and faith ; his spiritualistic as distinguished from materialistic Pantheism, the distinction which he tacitly draws between the Deity and external nature ; his sentimentalism, his fervid humanity, his sympathy—all, in fine, that makes and marks the *poet's heart*. From Platonism he adopts the use he has made of the doctrine of anamnesis, or the remembrance of what was experienced in a pre-existant state, and the doctrine of ideas or essence, as in the " Ode on the Intimations of Immortality," in the " Evening Ode," and in the sonnet which begins " I heard (alas ! 'twas only in a dream)," where the note proves his acquaintance with the " Phædo," while its sublime influence pervades his poems. We see it directly in his habitual employment of the term " shows," as in the " Poet's Epitaph " :

> The outward *shows* of sky and earth,
>   Of hill and valley, he has view'd ;
> And impulses of deeper birth
>   Have come to him in solitude.

And in that sublime passage in the " Excursion " :

> That what we feel of sorrow and despair
> From ruin and from change, and all the grief
> That passing *shows* of Being leave behind.*

---

* i. 948.

H

Or, again, where he speaks of " reading the *shows* of things with an unworthy eye." But I need not multiply instances. Platonism permeates his highest work, and, mixed with Stoicism, is in truth the basis of his metaphysics. Wordsworth's philosophy would have been quite possible without Stoicism ; as it is, it was probably altogether independent of it, but it would not have been possible without Platonism. Some people have tried to make out that Wordsworth was a Hegelian—he probably never read a line of Hegel in his life. Wordsworth was not a learned man ; he was one of the most original men who ever lived. All that he got from outsiders in the way of philosophy was probably—I say *probably*, because it is not known what he might have picked up from others, and from Coleridge particularly— a slight acquaintance with some of the Dialogues of Plato.

Was Wordsworth a Pantheist ? Certainly not, in the strict acceptation of the term. A Pantheist explains away, as the Stoics did, the existence of God by identifying him with matter ; but Wordsworth gives life and expression to matter by representing every object as full of God. True it is that Wordsworth's best and most characteristic work is entirely independent of Christianity, and could quite as well have been produced had Christianity never been. The " Lines on Tintern Abbey," " Laodamia," the " Ode on the Intimations," the " Ode to Duty," " The Happy Warrior," " Yarrow Revisited," and all such work as is essentially characteristic of him has more affinity with what is best in Paganism than in what is peculiar to Christianity. But he was, we know, a devout and strictly orthodox Christian, and it would probably have pained him to read what has just been written. But I should have had to tell him that I am writing not what I should like to write, but what I believe to be the truth ; and then, though he had not much sense of humour, he would very probably have smiled. He would have known that if we will only tell the truth about him he had not much to fear. Wordsworth, I repeat, was an orthodox Christian. When he heard that his enunciation of the doctrine of pre-existence had shocked some people, he wrote, " I think it right to protest against a conclusion which has given pain to some good and pious persons that I meant to inculcate such a belief. It is far too showy a notion to be recommended to faith," *but observe*, " as more than an element in our instincts of immortality." " But," he adds, " let us bear in mind that, though the idea is not advanced in revelation, there is nothing there to contradict it, and the fall of Man presents an analogy in its favour." He wrote, we must remember, the Ecclesiastical Sonnets, the Evening Voluntaries, the fifth, sixth, seventh and eighth books of the " Excursion," and those two beautiful poems the " Norman Boy " and the " Poet's Dream." Like Bishop Butler, Wordsworth pleaded that religion should " fix itself in form," and that great importance should be attached to ceremony and ritual. But no poet has expressed more beautifully the common sentiment of antiquity which the Stoic Seneca has put so well: " God is not to be worshipped by sacrifices and ceremonies, but by purity of life ; not in temples of stone, but in the shrine of the heart. Would you propitiate the gods ? Be good. We worship them best by imitating them."

He sees the bending multitude, He hears the choral rites,
Yet not the less in children's hymns and lonely prayer delights
God for His service needeth not proud works of human skill ;
They serve Him best who labour most to do in peace His will.*

In dealing with the Platonism of Wordsworth, especially in the great Ode, it is best not to press it too closely ; if we do, we shall be in danger of feeling that there are inconsistencies, and that positions are maintained which appear to contradict experience. We may smile, for example, at the apostrophe to the baby, and find it difficult to reconcile the commencement with the end of the Ode. But let us remember that such truths as are there embodied can only be expressed in symbol, and evade concrete expression just as they evade sensual apprehension. A sort of mid-point between what may be called the esotericism of the teaching and its popular intelligibleness would be afforded by Henry Vaughan's poem :

Happy those early days when I
Shin'd in my angel infancy !
.   .   .   .
When yet I had not walked above
A mile or two from my first Love,

---

* " The Poet's Dream."

> And looking back—at that short space—
> Could see a glimpse of His bright face ; *

and the lines which follow.

And now let me state categorically, as it were, the leading teachings of Wordsworth's philosophy, giving a few illustrations of each.

(1) That the material universe is not inert matter, but a vast living entity, endowed with sentient and intelligent life, having soul and reason; that the physical phenomena of the universe are to the soul of it what the body is to the soul of man ; that the same soul runs through all. This has been already illustrated.

(2) That the soul in man can be brought into harmony with the soul in Nature, and can, if properly trained, respond to the life of Nature and grow into intimate sympathy with her— that there is in it a majestic faculty, a purified imaginative power which can harmonise the thoughts, the feelings, the passions of men, elevating them above the regions of sensual dominion, above the clouds and mists of the body's life.

> Within the soul a faculty abides,
> That with interpositions, which would hide
> And darken, so can deal that they become
> Contingencies of pomp ; and serve to exalt
> Her native brightness. As the ample moon
> In the deep stillness of a summer even
> Rising behind a thick and lofty grove,

---

* " The Retreat."

> Burns, like an unconsuming fire of light,
> In the green trees ; and kindling on all sides
> Their leafy umbrage, turns the dusky veil
> Into a substance glorious as her own,
> Yea, with her own incorporated, by power
> Capacious and serene. Like power abides
> In man's celestial spirit ; virtue thus
> Sets forth and magnifies herself ; thus feeds
> A calm, a beautiful and silent fire,
> From the encumbrances of mortal life,
> From error, disappointment—nay from guilt ;
> And sometimes, so relenting justice wills,
> From palpable oppressions of despair.*

(3) That as man possesses the power of responding to Nature, possesses a soul which can be brought into harmony with the soul of Nature, he can be educated and moulded by Nature : she can lead him to peace and perfect contentment and satisfaction ; he can live her life, can be, as it were, one with her. This is the most purely beautiful and precious portion of Wordsworth's teaching, and it is exemplified in the poem beginning " Three years she grew in sun and shower " and in " Tintern Abbey," and again in the " Remembrance of Collins, composed upon the Thames near Richmond " :

> O glide, fair stream ! for ever so,
>   Thy quiet soul on all bestowing,
> Till all our minds for ever flow
>   As thy deep waters now are flowing.

So too the three poems on Yarrow, and the lines at the end of the first book of the " Excursion."

* " The Excursion," iv. 1058–77.

He has been hearing, you will remember, the sad story told by the old man, and is very sorrowful.

> Why then should we read
> The forms of things with an unworthy eye ?
> She sleeps in the calm earth, and peace is here.
> I well remember that those very plumes,
> Those weeds, and the high spear-grass on that wall,
> By mist and silent rain-drops silver'd o'er,
> As once I passed, into my heart conveyed
> So still an image of tranquillity,
> So calm and still and looked so beautiful
> Amid th' uneasy thoughts which fill'd my mind,
> That what we feel of sorrow and despair
> From ruin and from change, and all the grief
> That passing shows of Being leave behind,
> Appear'd an idle dream.

Once more, in the "Song at the Feast of Brougham Castle," when the good Lord Clifford was restored to his ancestors :

> Happy day, and mighty hour,
> When our Shepherd in his power,
> Mail'd and horsed, with lance and sword
> To his ancestors restored
> Like a reappearing Star,
> Like a glory from afar,
> First shall head the flock of war !

And so also of himself :

> If, in this time
> Of dereliction and dismay, I yet
> Despair not of our nature, but retain
> A more than Roman confidence, a faith
> That fails not, in all sorrow my support,
> The blessing of my life ; the gift is yours,
> Ye winds and sounding cataracts ! 'Tis yours,

> Ye mountains !   Thine, O Nature !   Thou hast fed
> My lofty speculations : and in thee,
> For this uneasy heart of ours, I find
> A never-failing principle of joy
> And purest passion.*

And he tells us too in what way this electric chord between the soul that is within us and the soul of the world is struck :

> There was a Boy ; ye knew him well, ye cliffs
> And islands of Winander ! many a time,
> At evening, when the earliest stars began
> To move along the edges of the hills,
> Rising or setting, would he stand alone
> Beneath the trees, or by the glimmering lake.
>
> .   .   .   .   .
>
> Then sometimes, in that silence, while he hung
> Listening, a gentle shock of mild surprise
> Has carried far into his heart the voice
> Of mountain torrents ; or the visible scene
> Would enter unawares into his mind.†

It is interesting to compare with this a passage in the Seventh Epistle of the " Pseudo Plato," sect. x. He is speaking of the intuition of idea or intellectual form.   He says it cannot be taught but from long converse with the thing itself, accompanied by a life in conformity to it—" On a sudden a light, as if from a leaping fire, will be enkindled in the soul and there nourish itself."

Wordsworth is always insisting on the necessity for man keeping himself as far as possible " pure and unspotted from the world " : if he would have

---

* " Prelude," Bk. II. 440–51.   † " There was a Boy."

nature, if he would have poetry be to him what they can be, he must wean himself from the gross and the material. We all know the sonnet, " The World is too much with us," but there is also a passage which deserves pondering over in one of his letters to Lady Beaumont : " It is an awful truth that there neither is nor can be any genuine enjoyment of poetry among nineteen out of twenty of those persons who live, or wish to live, in the broad light of the world ; among those who either are or are striving to make themselves people of consideration in society. This is a truth, and an awful one, because to be incapable of a feeling of poetry in my sense of the word is to be without love of human nature and reverence for God."*

As a moral teacher Wordsworth's teaching is closely linked with his spiritual, but three poems deserve special attention, and in all of these he is rigidly Stoical—" Laodamia " and the " Ode to Duty," the two sublimest moral poems in our literature, and " The Character of the Happy Warrior," that grand picture of the man

> Who if he be called upon to face
> Some awful moment to which Heav'n has joined
> Great issues, good or bad for human kind,
> Is happy as a Lover : and attired
> With sudden brightness, like a man inspired ;
> And, through the heat of conflict, keeps the law
> In calmness made, and sees what he foresaw.

" Laodamia " is the sort of poem which the first Brutus might have written. The point is the

* May 21, 1807.

subordination of the sensual to the spiritual, the subjection of passion to reason. Noble as the woman was—how noble we may gather from the sublime unselfishness of the praise she lavishes on the husband who preferred glory and honour to her love—she yet allows mere human affection to assert itself :

> Jove frown'd in heaven : the conscious Parcæ threw
> Upon those roseate lips a Stygian hue ;

and then again as Hermes appears to escort her husband to Hades, a passion of grief possesses her —the second sin.

> Thus, all in vain exhorted and reproved,
> She perished ; and as for a wilful crime,
> By the just Gods whom no weak pity mov'd,
> Was doom'd to wear out her appointed time,
> Apart from happy Ghosts, that gather flowers
> Of blissful quiet 'mid unfading bowers.
> Yet tears to human suffering are due.

And observe how not men only, but the trees on the tomb of Protesilaus pay a natural homage to the affections. The same lofty and austere morality animates the noble poem of " Dion." The " Ode to Duty " may similarly be compared with the Orphic "Hymn to Law."

Note too how he strips the tinsel off life, as well in his estimates as in his generalisations, " yielding homage only to eternal laws " : no conventional standards and touchstones are his.

And lastly let us notice his glorious optimism, his cheerful faith that all that we behold is full of blessings. This is perhaps his greatest charm as

a poet, the extraordinary power with which he feels
the joy offered to us in Nature, the joy offered to
us in the simple primary affections and duties, and
the extraordinary power with which in case after
case he makes us share it.

The poetry of Wordsworth is the reflection of
the most purely ideal life, rounded and complete in
all its harmonious proportions, of which biography
has record. No man was ever more nobly true
to himself or more completely fulfilled himself.
Sanity, purity, simplicity, sincerity, elevation
characterised the man, and characterise his
work. As we follow his career in the record of
his poems we see his powers broadening and
deepening and mellowing, as decade succeeds
decade. The perfervid enthusiasm of the days
when the

> Sounding cataract
> Haunted me like a passion : the tall rock,
> The mountain, and the deep and gloomy wood,
> Their colours and their forms were then to me
> An appetite ; a feeling and a love
> That had no need of a remoter charm,[*]

passes into the calmer moods, when he had
learnt

> To look on Nature, not as in the hour
> Of thoughtless youth ; but hearing oftentimes
> The still, sad music of humanity,[†]

on to the maturer years when

[*] " Tintern Abbey," 76.   [†] Ibid. 89.

The clouds that gather round the setting sun
Do take a sober colouring from an eye
That hath kept watch o'er man's mortality.*

And then we see him as an old man, solitary amid
the memories of the past,

When last along its banks I wandered
  Through groves that had begun to shed
Their golden leaves upon the pathways,
  My steps the Border-minstrel led.
The mighty Minstrel breathes no longer,
  'Mid mouldering ruins low he lies ;
And death upon the braes of Yarrow
  Has closed the Shepherd-poet's eyes.
Nor has the rolling year twice measur'd
  From sign to sign its steadfast course,
Since every mortal power of Coleridge
  Was frozen at its marvellous source.
The rapt One of the godlike forehead,
  The heaven-eyed creature sleeps in earth ;
And Lamb, the frolic and the gentle
  Has vanished from his lonely hearth.
Like clouds that rake the mountain-summits
  Or waves that own no curbing hand,
How fast has brother follow'd brother
  From sunshine to the sunless land.

. . . . .

Our haughty life is crown'd with darkness—†

But what of all this to one to whom all was but

A windswept-meadow
  Mimicking a troubled sea,
Such is life ; and death a shadow
From the rock eternity ‡

---

* "Ode to Immortality," xi.
† "On the Death of James Hogg."
‡ "Hermit's Cell."

—all here but as the " passing shows of being " ?
How perfect was the close ! How in the " Yarrow
Revisited " is the whole of life contemplated
through an atmosphere by which *all* is reconciled
and harmonised.

Had he not learned to look on nature and man
as each is contemplated in the epilogue to the
Duddon Sonnets ?

> I see what was, and is, and will abide ;
> Still glides the Stream and shall for ever glide ;
> The Form remains, the Function never dies ;
> While we the brave, the mighty and the wise,
> We *men*, who in our morn of youth defied
> The elements, must vanish ;—be it so !
> Enough, if something from our hands have power
> To live, and act, and serve the future hour ;
> And if, as toward the silent tomb we go,
> Through love, through hope and faith's transcendent dower,
> We feel that we are greater than we know.

Of all this and of how much more is his poetry
the record. How immense, how incalculable is
our debt to him ! It may be said of him as of the
poet whom he loved so reverently, Spenser, that
he has consecrated life by revealing and interpreting its dignity, its beauty, its importance. It
would hardly be exaggeration to say that we
cannot see the sun shine or look on any of nature's
works with the same eyes as before he spoke.
How better can we take our leave of him than in
the lines in which another poet addressed a spirit
power ?

> Thy voice is on the rolling air ;
> I hear thee where the waters run ;

Thou standest in the rising sun,
And in the setting thou art fair.

. . .

Far off thou art, but ever nigh ;
I have thee still, and I rejoice ;
I prosper, circled with thy voice ;
I shall not lose thee tho' I die.*

It is interesting to compare what may be called the last message of three of the world's greatest poets—the record of the completed vision. They are to be found in the " Œdipus Coloneus " of Sophocles, " The Tempest " of Shakespeare, the " Yarrow Revisited " of Wordsworth, and they deliver the same message, which in its general conclusion Tennyson has so beautifully summarised :

And all is well,—tho' faith and form
Be sunder'd in the night of fear ;
Well roars the storm to those that hear
A deeper voice above the storm.†

---

* Tennyson's " In Memoriam," cxxx.   † Ibid. cxxvii.

EMERSON

O monstrous dead, unprofitable world
That thou canst hear and, hearing, hold thy way,
A voice oracular hath peal'd to-day ;
To-day a hero's banner is unfurl'd :

Hast thou no lip for welcome ?—So I said.
Man after man the world smil'd and passed by,
A smile of wistful incredulity
As though one spoke of life unto the dead—

Scornful, and strange, and sorrowful, and full
Of bitter knowledge.   Yet the will is free ;
Strong is the soul, and wise and beautiful :
The seeds of godlike power are in us still :
Gods are we, bards, saints, heroes if we will !
Dumb judges, answer, truth or mockery ?

SO wrote Matthew Arnold when he was a young man in a volume of Emerson's Essays, and when he was in the maturity of his powers, not very long before he passed away, he said deliberately : "As Wordsworth's poetry is, in my judgment, the most important work done in verse, in our language, during the present century, so Emerson's Essays are, I think, the most important work done in prose." * And yet in the same address in which he had thus expressed himself he has excluded Emerson from a place among the great writers,

* "Discourses in America : Emerson,"

the great men of letters —and he gives us types,
Cicero, Plato, Bacon, Pascal, Swift, Voltaire.
What does he mean then by saying that Emerson's
work in prose is the most important work done
in prose in the nineteenth century ? This is a
question into which we must presently inquire,
for it takes us into the very heart of our subject.
And beside this testimony of Matthew Arnold
let us place that of an eminent countryman of
Emerson. Theodore Parker used to say that he
thanked God for three things particularly—" the
sun, the moon, and Ralph Waldo Emerson." And
Emerson had this distinction also, that he shared
with Goethe the honour of being the only man
in the nineteenth century who fascinated Carlyle.

Here, surely, then, we have a remarkable and
most memorable man, whether he appeals to us
or not—and to many of us he will not appeal : to
many a cultivated and intelligent man and woman
his work will mean very little, it will even, perhaps,
ring false ; to many his volumes will be a very
Barmecide's Feast. Emerson is the apostle—it
would, perhaps, be begging an important question
to say the author of a gospel—the seer and
promulgator of ideas, or truths so exalted and
divine, so essentially transcendental, that they
may be compared to the Holy Grail. Nor would
it be fanciful to compare those who explore
Emerson's volumes for his spiritual message, that
they may take it for their guide, with those who,
in Tennyson's poem, set out on the quest of the
Grail. You remember their fortunes. Two see
it, Galahad, perfect purity, and Percival, perfect

holiness, and both are lost to the world and pass respectively into the Spiritual Kingdom and into contemplative seclusion : honest, plain Sir Bors gets a cheering glimpse of it while imprisoned ; Launcelot sees it, but, half-blinded and half-distracted, sees it veiled ; Gawain soon gives up the quest, takes to frivolities, and sees it not at all. Now I had better confess at once that my fortune in the quest of the Emersonian Grail has been partly that of Sir Bors and partly that of Sir Launcelot. The reader's fortunes will also, no doubt, vary according to temperament and according to sympathy and taste. Some will perhaps enjoy with Galahad and Percival the full vision, but all I can do is to start you fairly on the quest.

How the student of Emerson is likely to fare, as well as the reasons of his thus faring, are so clearly indicated by Emerson himself that I cannot do better than quote the passage at once, as the best way of opening the subject. In his lecture on "The Transcendentalist" he thus writes. He begins by saying that what is popularly called transcendentalism is idealism, and he prefers the terms idealism and idealists to transcendentalism and transcendentalists, and then continues :

As thinkers mankind have ever divided into two sects, materialists and idealists : the first class founded on experience, the second on consciousness ; the first class beginning to think from the data of the senses, the second class perceive that the senses are not final, and say the senses give us representations of things, but what are the things themselves they cannot tell. The materialist insists on facts, on history, on the force of circumstances, and the animal wants of man ; the idealist on the power of Thought and of Will, on inspiration, on miracle, on individual

I

culture. . . . The materialist takes his departure from the external world and esteems a man as one product of that; the idealist takes his departure from his consciousness, and reckons the world an appearance. . . . His thought, that is the Universe.

Emerson is pre-eminently and essentially an idealist; he surveys everything—man, mankind, nature, the universe, all that pertains to the human, all that pertains to the divine—from the ideal point of view; his touchstone is the ideal, his standard is the ideal—what is material and carnal, what is anthropomorphic, is with him mere dross. And in this spirit we must study him : to the materialist he will be simply unintelligible or absurd. What reason is in the study of most other philosophers, sympathy and sympathetic insight are in the study of Emerson. Wordsworth says of his poet, " You must love him e'er to you he will seem worthy of your love," and of Emerson this is equally true. Our appreciation of him will be in exact proportion to our capacity of sympathy. Without such sympathy much of his most characteristic teaching will be unintelligible, will be simple rhapsody. That sympathy, therefore, if we do not already possess it, we must acquire. And it is not difficult to acquire it. In the first place, the personality of Emerson is a singularly attractive one. The philosopher of the ideal illustrated it in his character and in his life. Sincere and modest, benevolent and gentle, all who knew him loved him, and all who loved revered him, for, indifferent to ambition and the world's rewards, and wholly unselfish, he dedicated himself, like Socrates, to the ungrateful task of attempting to kindle spiritual life in "a great, intelligent, sensual, avaricious people," and to the disinterested and single-hearted pursuit of truth and virtue. Secondly, however unintelligible, however unsatisfactory if you like, much of his esoteric philosophy may be, he re-interpreted for the modern world, in language which all can understand, great, inspiring, illumining, consoling truths which deeply concern and come home to all of us, and he preached with most impressive power, lucidity, and eloquence a gospel sorely needed in these latter days — the gospel of cheerfulness and courage, of hopeful patience, of confidence that the Power to which we owe our instincts and our aspirations will not suffer those instincts and aspirations to be frustrate. And, thirdly, his writings, both in verse and in prose, sparkle with gems of thought, of sentiment, of expression which arrest and charm at once and for ever, which, once read, are never forgotten. Such, to give one example in verse and one in prose, would be:

> So nigh is grandeur to our dust,
> So near to God is man,
> When Duty whispers low, *Thou must*,
> The youth replies, *I can;* *

and

That which befits us, embosomed in beauty and wonder as we are, is cheerfulness and courage and the endeavour to realise our aspirations. Shall not the heart which has received so much trust the Power by which it lives? †

---

* "Voluntaries," iii.   † "New England Reformers."

To the ancestry, parents, and surroundings, using the word in its most comprehensive sense, of men of genius are almost always to be traced not only the general characteristics of their genius but the explanation of the turn it took. And Emerson was no exception. He was descended from a long line of earnest and serious preachers. One of his ancestors was the Rev. Peter Bulkeley, rector of Woodhill, in Bedfordshire, and Fellow of St. John's College, Cambridge, who, in consequence of Laud's persecutions of the Nonconformists, emigrated to New England in 1634. He was one of the fathers of Nonconformity in America, and was the author of a celebrated work, " Gospel Covenant," one of the sentiments in which anticipates a leading tenet of his illustrious descendant : " The Church is built on the foundations of prophets and apostles, not in regard of their persons but of their doctrines." His grandfather built the Old Manse of Concord, celebrated by Hawthorne, and was a chaplain in the army which fought for independence, dying in 1776. His father, a very eloquent preacher and a locally distinguished man of letters, in whom we trace many of the characteristics of the son, was pastor of the first Unitarian Church at Boston. Of his mother nothing remarkable is recorded, but she was a serious, pious, good woman. Ralph Waldo was born May 25, 1803, at Boston, within a kite-string's distance of the birthplace of Benjamin Franklin. His father died prematurely eight years later, leaving Mrs. Emerson very ill provided

for with six children, all under ten years of age·
She brought up her children well under the
severe discipline of poverty, so that they had to
work as servants, chopping wood, lighting fires,
and doing what they could to help their mother.
Thus was young Emerson strengthened in fru-
gality and self-denial by what he describes as the
iron hand of poverty, of necessity, of austerity.
He was a serious and thoughtful child, early
encouraged to read good books—Shakespeare,
Milton, Addison, and the like—by his aunt, Mary
Moody Emerson. This aunt must certainly be
reckoned among the formative influences of
Emerson's life. He said himself many years
afterwards: " She must always occupy a saint's
place in my household; and I have no hour of
poetry or philosophy, since I knew these things,
into which she does not enter as a genius." She
was a curious " saint," for she was a woman of a
most imperious temper, alternately grim and
rigid, and most affectionate and tender: partly a
tenaciously conservative Puritan, and partly in
responsive sympathy with the new ideas. As a
boy, and at school, Emerson came perilously near
to being a prig, being, we are told, quite faultless,
never joining in games and amusements, keeping
to himself, and most studious and quietly
observant, but without any airs of superiority
and without any conceit, and so, whatever may
have been the proximity, not a prig.

In August 1817 he entered Harvard University.
Here he in no way distinguished himself: he
seems to have shirked the serious study of serious

subjects, and chiefly employed his time in what may be called contemplatively lounging and reading such books as interested him, and they were always good books, such as Chaucer, Shakespeare, Swift, Addison, Sterne, and Plutarch and Montaigne in translations; of the classics in the original he knew next to nothing, and never made himself a scholar. In April 1824 he began to read to qualify himself for the ministry.

> I am [he wrote] beginning my professional studies: in a month I shall be legally a man. I cannot dissemble that my abilities are below my ambition. I have or had a strong imagination and consequently a keen relish for the beauties of poetry. My reasoning faculty is proportionately weak, nor can I ever hope to write a Butler's "Analogy" or an essay of Hume. I burn after the *aliquid immensum infinitumque* which Cicero desired.

And this indicates that Emerson had at least one of the attributes of genius as distinguished from talent—he took correctly his own measure. It was not a good start in life, this loose and desultory education, and it cannot be disguised that Emerson's work has been most seriously affected by it. It is this want of discipline and severe systematic training which makes such a gulf between Emerson and the classics of Philosophy. He speaks himself of "his cardinal vice of intellectual dissipation, sinful strolling from book to book, from care to idleness"—"a malady that belongs," he adds, "to the chapter of incurables."

After taking his degree he taught for some months in a school, reading meanwhile in Divinity that he might qualify himself for a licence to preach. He was approbated, as it was

called, in October 1826, and on the 10th of that
month preached his first sermon.   After remaining a year at Divinity Hall he became the ordained
colleague of Henry Ware, pastor of the second
Unitarian Church of Boston, and shortly afterwards succeeded Ware as sole incumbent.   This
is the beginning of Emerson's public career.

And now he began seriously to think for himself, and gradually to formulate the opinions and
doctrines of which he was to become the prophet.
The crisis came in 1832 when, on conscientious
grounds, he resigned his pastorate.   As pastor he
had to celebrate the rite of the Lord's Supper in
the sense of regarding it as a sacrament established
by Christ and in His name by the Church.   As a
sacrament he could not regard or celebrate it ; he
was willing to continue the service provided the
rite was regarded as merely one of commemora-
tion.   To this the committee appointed by the
congregation would not submit, and Emerson
therefore resigned his cure.   His explanation of
his objection is so significant and characteristic
that it may be quoted :

The use of the elements, however suitable to the people and
the modes of thought in the East, where it originated, is foreign
and unsuited to affect us. . . . The Jewish was a religion of
forms ; it was all body, it had no life, and the Almighty God was
pleased to qualify and send forth a man to teach men that they
must serve Him with the heart ; that only that life was religious
which was thoroughly good ; that sacrifice was smoke and forms
were shadows. This man lived and died true to this purpose ;
and now with His blessed word and life before us, Christians must
contend that it is a matter of vital importance—really a duty—to
commemorate Him by a certain form, whether that form be

agreeable to their understandings or not. Is not this to make vain the gift of God ? Is not this to turn back the hand on the dial ? *

The truth is that Emerson had convinced himself of what is embodied in his own saying, " Let every man be his own Church "; that all forms of faith, whether Christian or Pagan, whether Calvinist or Unitarian, are merely versions, so to speak, of the Moral Law; that if men are to be saved they cannot be saved miraculously or vicariously, but by their own God-directed efforts. It was a serious step for him to take, and the anxiety involved in it was complicated by the distress occasioned by the death of his wife, whom he had married about two years before.

His health was seriously affected, and a voyage to Europe was recommended. So on Christmas Day 1832 he sailed for Europe. Of this visit to Europe he has given a short but vivid account in the first chapter of his "English Traits." In Italy he met Landor ; in London, Coleridge ; at the Lakes, Wordsworth, who told him that he thought Carlyle was sometimes insane ; at Craigenputtock, Carlyle, this same Carlyle who was sometimes insane—and this was his most memorable experience. The two men laid the foundation of an intimate lifelong acquaintance which has its record in the Correspondence edited by C. E. Norton, the first letter being

* " The Lord's Supper." From his sermon on resigning his pastorate, delivered September 9, 1832. He took his text from Romans xiv. 17 : " The kingdom of God is not meat and drink ; but righteousness and peace and joy in the Holy Ghost."

dated May 14, 1834, the last April 1872. There
was much in Emerson's nature and temperament
which went out to meet Carlyle. Carlyle was
the more potent spirit, but Emerson was no
idolator, nor can he be called even a disciple of
Carlyle : though mutually attracted, each moved
in his own orbit.

Emerson returned to America with his health
re-established, his mind enlarged, his powers
rapidly maturing, his convictions confirmed and
hardened into fanaticism :

> I thank the Great God [he wrote in his diary] who has led
> me through this great European scene, this last school-room in
> which He has pleased to instruct me. He has thereby comforted
> and confirmed me in my convictions. Many things I owe to the
> sight of these men.

But what he had learnt he had learnt negatively—
the limitations of the great, the littleness of the
famous ; he had learnt that fame is a conventional
thing, that man is a sadly limitary spirit : he had
learnt the folly of " prematurely canonising."

In 1835 he married again and settled at Concord,
in the Coolidge house, a peaceful, beautiful spot,
where he remained to the end of his days. The
house in which he lived, let us note in passing,
is Hawthorne's Old Manse in which was written
" Mosses from an Old Manse." And now
Emerson's career began in real earnest ; it was
initiated by a great sorrow—the death of his
beloved brother Charles ; in such sorrow is the
baptism of genius unto spiritual power, for is
it not truthfully written ?

> Who ne'er his bread in sorrow ate,
> Who ne'er the mournful midnight hours,
> Weeping upon his bed has sate,
> He knows you not, ye Heavenly Powers.*

To 1836, 1837, and 1838 belong Emerson's three most comprehensively characteristic works, the works which at once initiated and fulfilled, at least in embryo, his gospel to his countrymen and to the world. The first was a little book of less than a hundred small pages, entitled " Nature," which may be described as a mystic prose poem, or rhapsody, in eight chapters. "It is," says Holmes, " a kind of New England Genesis in place of the Old Testament one." " I call it," says Carlyle, " the foundation and ground-plan on which you may build whatsoever of great and true that has been given you to build." And this it verily was, and on this foundation Emerson did build ever afterwards. The next performance was " The American Scholar," an oration delivered before the Phi-Beta Kappa Society, at Cambridge, August 31, 1837. This was a trumpet-call to young America. Its note is struck at the opening :

Our day of dependence, our long apprenticeship to the learning of other lands, draws to a close. The millions that around us are rushing into life cannot always be fed on the sere remains of foreign harvests. Events, actions arise that must be sung, that will sing themselves. Who can doubt that poetry will revive and lead in a new age, as the star in the constellation Harp, which now flames in our zenith, astronomers announce shall one day be the pole-star for a thousand years ?

---

* Longfellow's " Motto, Hyperion," Bk. I.

It is a plea for spiritual and intellectual emancipation, for generous liberal culture. The great destinies of the future are in the hands of the " scholar "—not the scholar as the past understood the word, but as the future must understand it, the scholar as representing a man

who must take up into himself all the ability of the time, all the contributions of the past, all the hopes of the future. He must be a university of knowledges.

He must represent the full development, not of one or two, but of all man's faculties and capacities. He must not be the slave of tradition and authority: he must not anchor in the past: he must sail onward in the present to the future. And he concludes in summary:

We will walk on our own feet: we will work with our own hands: we will speak our own minds. The study of letters shall be no longer a name for pity, for doubt, and for sensual indulgence. The dread of man and the love of man shall be a wall of defence and a wreath of joy around all. A nation of men will for the first time exist, because each believes himself inspired by the Divine Soul which also inspires all men.

Such was the oration which Lowell calls " an event without any former parallel in American literary annals," and which Holmes describes as " our intellectual Declaration of Independence."

Emerson's third memorable discourse was " An Address before the Senior Class in Divinity College, Cambridge," delivered on Sunday evening, July 15, 1838. In this he dealt as freely and boldly with religion as in the former discourse he had with education. It was a plea for the broadest latitudinarianism, a plea for private right of judgment as against all historical creeds, bibles, churches—exalting individual consciousness above all authority, making the individual soul supreme arbiter in spiritual matters: a plea for absolute spiritual emancipation. Without bitterness or levity, without any irreverence, he takes exception to historical Christianity, because he says it exaggerates the personal, the positive, the ritual, because it monopolises what is general and common. It assumes, he complains, that the age of inspiration is past; that the Bible is closed; that God "was" rather than "is"—that He "spake," not that He "is speaking." He complains that the doctrine of inspiration is lost, and that the base doctrine of the majority of voices usurps the place of the doctrine of the soul.

Great exception was taken to this discourse, and his former colleague, Ware, both wrote and preached against it. Emerson's letter to him in reply is an example of his modest and amiable, but at the same time firm and uncompromising temper.

And now, as I have explained Emerson's position and work when he was fully started on his career, we may pause for a moment to glance at his surroundings and at what had preceded his appearance. The chief activity in America was mercantile, the general tone and character of life and society grossly material. Absorbed in business pursuits, the majority cared nothing for culture, or indeed for anything which was not

conducive to what was called practical success.
Higher education was scarcely in its infancy. A
national literature could hardly be said to exist.
What literature existed was imitative and commonplace, modelled on that of the Old World.
In religion Puritanism prevailed, and Puritanism
was as hostile to belles lettres, philosophy, and
art as the coarser Philistinism of the mart,
exchange, and workshop. While public life was
industrial and utilitarian, private life stagnated in
dull and colourless conventionality. But signs of
a reaction were at hand. In religion Unitarianism
had been for some time gaining ground, but it
had as little vitalising power as its grimmer rival.
In 1815 was started the *North American Review*,
and with this review the dawn of American
literature broke. Among Emerson's predecessors
may be specified his Divinity teacher, Dr. Channing, one of the most eloquent of American
pulpit orators and writers, and William Cullen
Bryant, whose two poems, "Thanatopsis" and the
" Forest Hymn," fairly entitle him to the honour
of being called the American Wordsworth, and
whose essay and "Popular History of the United
States" give him a distinguished place among
masters of prose. The greatest names in American
literature—Edgar Allan Poe, Longfellow, Hawthorne, Prescott, Lowell, Motley—were his contemporaries, and among his audience.

The transcendental movement with which
Emerson is so prominently associated had defined
itself before his earliest writings appeared. It
was the result partly of the inevitable reaction

against materialism, partly of the peculiar conditions of the time. A passion for facts, for what is intelligible and tangible, for what can be formularised and presented definitely and concretely, had come into collision with the powers which were dissolving the old régime. Criticism was beginning to demolish the bases of the Old Religion; science was becoming restlessly active. The long dominion of Puritanism had induced a serious, earnest spirit, and though it had ceased to satisfy the intellectual and spiritual needs of men, it had prepared them to welcome an attempt to reconstruct life on an ideal basis. And so it was that all that was tending in this direction throughout Europe became influential in America—the wild and extravagant visions of Swedenborg, the cloudy reveries of Coleridge, the noble idealism of Wordsworth, the new bases for speculation supplied by philosophers like Kant, Fichte, Schelling, the intense spiritualism of Richter, Novalis—all that Schiller, all that Goethe, all that Herder had contributed to the widening of the intellectual and spiritual horizon. Nor must we omit Carlyle, who just before Emerson had begun his career had published his essay on " Characteristics " and his " Signs of the Times " as well as his " Sartor Resartus." *   Of this movement Emerson, after the publication of the works to which I have referred, became the acknowledged leader, became *the* prophet, *the* apostle. And he led not merely by virtue of the power and eloquence of his addresses, lectures, and writings,

* *Fraser Magazine,* 1833–34.

but by the influence and charm of his personal
character and example. His simplicity, his sincerity, his unselfish devotion to the work which he
had set himself to do appealed to every one.
" His words had power," says Hawthorne, " because they accorded with his thoughts, and his
thoughts had reality and depth because they
harmonised with the life that he always lived."
Emerson never " posed," was never aggressive ;
he was always reverent, he was always modest,
he never argued, a serene smile was all that
an opponent as a rule got from him as reply.
And all felt his personal charm. He had, as the
Spanish phrase so beautifully puts it, a face like a
blessing. For forty years he lectured and published lectures, "peddling out," he said, "all the
wit I can gather from Time or from Nature, and
am pained at heart to see how thankfully that
little is received." As a lecturer and writer he
was very poorly paid, and was never in easy circumstances till he was nearly seventy years old ; but
he never complained, he practised what he
preached : " plain living and high thinking."

An epoch in the history of the movement led
by Emerson was marked in July 1840 by the
establishment of *The Dial*, a magazine which
continued to appear quarterly till April 1844.
For the first two years it was edited by that most
remarkable woman Margaret Fuller, and after
April 1842 by Emerson. Here the transcendentalists gave expression to their faith in ideas,
their reactionary protests against the doctrines of
the philosophy of the senses, their strenuous

assertion of the principle that the forms of one age are inadequate to express the wants of another, their contention that it is not in commercial and material prosperity but in spiritual and intellectual activity that human success and man's true beatitude consist. Its spirit was catholic and cosmopolitan—all the creeds of the world were canvassed and criticised ; philosophic works were reviewed. It illustrates all that is best and all that is most extravagant in the movement. Emerson extensively contributed, so also did Theodore Parker, Alcott, Ripley, and Thoreau. Carlyle wrote :

> I love your *Dial* and yet it is with a kind of shudder. You seem to me in danger of dividing yourselves from the Fact of the present Universe, in which alone, ugly as it is, can I find any anchorage, and soaring away after Ideas, Beliefs, Revelations, and such like—into perilous altitudes as I think ; beyond the curve of perpetual frost, for one thing ! I know not how to utter what impression you give me.[*]

Another result of the transcendental movement was the famous Brook Farm experiment, founded in 1842 by George Ripley. It was an attempt to reconcile labour, capital, and culture, partly based on Fourierism and partly on the general impulse to universal reform. In a letter written in 1841 Dr. Channing had said: " I have for a long time dreamed of an association in which the members, instead of preying on one another, after the fashion of this world, should live together as brothers, seeking one another's elevation and spiritual growth." This was to be realised.

[*] Letter dated August 29, 1842.

A farm of about two hundred acres was purchased in West Roxbury, about nine miles from Boston—a most charming spot. The original pioneers were about twenty, growing at last, when the fullest number was reached, to 150. Every one was to labour at some trade or give some equivalent in labour for the privilege of belonging to the community: a fair price would be paid for that labour, which would thus purchase leisure to live in all the faculties of the soul. The highest activity of the settlement was education, and there were teachers in almost every subject. These teachers found recreation in such useful pursuits as pleased them —farming, gardening, or some other branch cf domestic service. Ripley himself, for example, who taught intellectual and moral philosophy and mathematics, liked to milk cows, finding such occupation favourable to contemplation, " particularly when the cow's tail was looped up behind "; or he would help to clean out the stables because he found sordid and dirty work done against the grain conducive to moral improvement, to say nothing of its usefulness. The religion of the place was absolutely cosmopolitan. Every one could believe what he pleased, and practise the rites of his creed if he had any. Some were Swedenborgians ; one died in the Episcopal faith and was buried in accordance with its rites ; many were Unitarians—but all called themselves Christians because all reverenced the character and example of Christ. In fact, the ideal was to lead a pure, moral, useful,

K

healthy life, untrammelled by any creeds, any forms of intellectual, political, and social coercion beyond what respect for the higher self and the interests of humanity imposed. Ripley did all in his power to induce Emerson to join a community some of the leading principles of which he had done so much to inspire. But he resolutely declined, and his letter to Ripley illustrates that shrewd and practical good sense which generally underlay his most extravagant transcendentalism. He had owned that it was a noble and generous movement on the part of its projectors to try an experiment of better living, but he writes :

> I am in many respects placed as I wish to be. I cannot accuse my townsmen or my neighbours of my domestic grievances. It seems to me a circuitous and obverse way of relieving myself to put upon your community the emancipation which I ought to take upon myself. The institution of hired service is to me very disagreeable. I should like to come one step nearer nature than this usage permits. But surely I need not sell my house and remove my family to Newton in order to make the experiment of labour and self-help. I am already in the act of trying some domestic and social experiments which would gain nothing.

So tactfully and so courteously did he waive Brook Farm aside. And indeed he had important work to do. The establishment of *The Dial* and what culminated in the Brook Farm experiment had the effect of leading to movements which reduced transcendentalism to an absurdity. In 1840 and 1841 a convention for universal reform was assembled at Chardon Street, Boston, and a most motley group it was, consisting, in Emerson's own words, of

madmen, madwomen, men with beards, Dunkers, Muggle-
tonians, Come-outers, Groaners, Agrarians, Seventh-Day Baptists,
Quakers, Abolitionists, Calvinists, Unitarians, and Philosophers.

His hope was in young America ; his task was
to control and discipline the enthusiasm excited.
He preached against extravagance and the abuse
of energy, inculcating that it was more true and
noble to *live* than to theorise and speculate ; he
discountenanced the withdrawal from public and
domestic duties. He pointed out that there was
practical work to do " while the colossal wrongs of
the Indian, of the negro, of the emigrant remained
unmitigated, and the religious, civil, and judicial
forms of the country are confessedly effete and
offensive." In 1841 he published the first
volume of his collected essays—it contained two
of his most extravagant, namely, " Over-Soul "
and " Circles "; two of his wisest, " Self-Reliance "
and " Compensation "; one of his most poetical,
" Love." In January 1842 a great sorrow befell
him, a sorrow which haunted his life, the loss of
his dear little son, his eldest son, who was only
five years old. Nearly the last connected words
which he spoke on his own death-bed forty-one
years later were, " Oh, that beautiful boy ! " and
this loss inspired his poem, the " Threnody."

In 1844 he delivered the address " The Young
American," in which he, the most American of
Americans, exhorted the Americans to be Americans, to develop on their own lines, to fulfil
themselves :

If only the men are employed in conspiring with the designs
of the Spirit who led us hither and is leading us still, we shall

quickly enough advance out of all hearing of others' censures, out of all regrets of our own, into a new and more excellent social state than history has recorded.

The delivery of this address was succeeded by the publication of his second collection of essays. The most remarkable essays in the volume are "Character," "Manners," and "Gifts"; but two are of particular interest as throwing light on his relation to his country and his countrymen, viz. "Politics" and "New England Reformers." In Emerson may be said to have been combined many of the characteristics of Berkeley, Wordsworth, and Franklin, and whenever he deals with social and political questions in their practical aspect comes out invariably the *Franklin side of him*— shrewdness, level-headedness, common-sense. In politics he had no confidence either in the Democrats or in the Conservatives, whose characteristics he admirably analyses. "The New England Reformers" is an equally admirable commentary on the virtues and defects of the transcendentalists and reformers. Though he had the greatest sympathy with their ideals, sympathy never misled him.

In 1847 Emerson, having been invited to give a series of lectures before the Mechanics' Institutes of the Northern and Midland Counties, sailed for England in October of that year.

His experiences, the friends he made, the great men he met, he has himself recorded in a series of notes which on his return to America he expanded into lectures, and afterwards published in the most concrete and popular of his books—" English

Traits." Over Emerson's judgments on England and the English we need not pause. He certainly found no heroes among us, and no studies for a social and political Utopia. He praises what all the world has praised in us, and makes such deductions as a man of his temper and ideals would be likely to make. He was a genial and kindly observer, but as a delineator and critic given to exaggeration and somewhat loose in his assertions and generalisations.

On his return to America he had added very little, if anything, to his stock of ideas, and not a touch of Anglicism modified his essentially American temper: his cosmopolitanism had perhaps become more confirmed, but that is all that can be said. From the lectures which he delivered in England, which were no doubt suggested by Carlyle's "Heroes and Hero Worship," he selected some for publication. They make up what he calls his "Representative Men": Plato, Swedenborg, Montaigne, Shakespeare, Napoleon, Goethe. As criticisms of these great men his lectures are, it is needless to say, mere absurdities, save here and there for flashes of penetrating insight. Each represents a congeries of ideas, of intensely Emersonian ideas, and on these he discourses. But they are full of inspiration, fertilisingly suggestive. Nowhere has Emerson preached his gospel with more eloquence and emphasis. He says in the opening address on the uses of great men:

Within the limits of human education and agency, we may say, great men exist that there may be greater men ;

and on this text he preaches. Reading these essays is like receiving a series of galvanic shocks, and the reader is fortunate if he does not emerge from their perusal a nervously mental wreck.

Of personal details little remains to be told. A central figure in a society the members of which were some of the most brilliant representatives of American literature, revered and beloved by a large circle, incessantly lecturing and writing, in every way furthering the cause of Truth, Justice, and Liberty as he conceived them, though cautiously refraining from all association with extravagance and abuse, his life glided on to honoured old age. The steady and vehement friend of negro emancipation, he was on the side of the Northerners in the war, having before proposed to buy the slaves from the planters for two thousand millions, which he, poor visionary, thought would be enthusiastically subscribed. A third visit to Europe in 1872, in which he saw for the last time his old friend Carlyle, preceded the final decade of his long life. He was much gratified by the honours and recognition given him by Harvard University, and for his nomination in 1874 for the Lord Rectorship of Glasgow, where he obtained five hundred votes against Lord Beaconsfield's seven hundred. His life had been so full and so vigorously energetic that as years advanced he found it difficult to realise that he was getting old. In one of his poems, " Terminus," he gives beautiful expression to the resignation and tranquillity with which he accepted the inevitable :

> As the bird trims her to the gale,
> I trim myself to the storm of time,
> I man the rudder, reef the sail,
> Obey the voice at eve obeyed at prime :
> " Lowly faithful, banish fear,
> Right onward drive unharmed :
> The port, well worth the cruise, is near,
> And every wave is charmed."

As long as his faculties served him he continued to be usefully busy on the platform and with his pen, protesting against utilitarian ethics, against materialism in philosophy, against formality in religion, against blind submission to tradition and authority. His decline was gradual and placid. Latterly his memory entirely failed him as to facts and details, and though it had never been accurate with regard to them, it had done him loyal service. Impressions were what he valued, ideas were everything to him ; facts and particulars mere husks. O. W. Holmes tells a characteristic and pathetic anecdote illustrating this. " The last time I saw him living," he says, " was at Longfellow's funeral. I was sitting opposite to him, when he rose and, going to the side of the coffin, looked intently upon the face of the dead poet. A few minutes later he rose again, and looked once more on the familiar features, not apparently remembering that he had just done so. Then he said to a friend near him : ' That gentleman was a sweet beautiful soul, but I have entirely forgotten his name.' "

He died on April 27, 1882, in his eightieth year, and we cannot better take our leave of him than in his own words, for in those words, we may be sure, he would have wished us to take our leave of him:

> Voice of earth to earth returned,
> Prayers of Saints that inly burned,—
> Saying, *What is excellent*
> *As God lives, is permanent;*
> *Hearts are dust, heart's loves remain,*
> *Heart's love will meet thee again.*
>
> *　　*　　*　　*　　*
>
> House and tenant go to ground,
> Lost in God, in Godhead found.*

---

* " Threnody."

EMERSON'S WRITINGS

IN Emerson's writings there is no system, and if we except the loose unity of certain leading and all-pervading ideas and teachings, no unity. He has left no great work, no work which sums up or comprehensively illustrates his philosophy. Everything he has left in prose resolves itself into lectures and essays; in verse, into short lyrics or epigrams. Tabulated his writings may be thus arranged. First, the little treatise, or, as it might be more properly described, the reflective prose poem, entitled "Nature," in eight sections, the most mystic and extravagant of all his writings. Secondly, the orations and addresses, the most remarkable of which are "The American Scholar," a trumpet-note to the Americans to awake from intellectual and spiritual torpor, to trust themselves and become spiritually and intellectually what they could and ought to become; "An Address to the Senior Class in Divinity College, Cambridge," "a plea for the individual consciousness as against all historical creeds, bibles, churches—a plea for the soul as the supreme judge in spiritual matters" (Holmes); "Literary Ethics," a plea for emancipation, self-reliance, sincerity, and the disinterested pursuit of truth; "Man the Reformer," a very noble oration the key to which is:

We are to revise the whole of our social structure, the state, the school, religion, marriage, trade, science, and explore their foundations in our own nature : we are to see that the world not only fitted the former men but fits us, and to clear ourselves of every usage which has not its roots in our own mind. What is a man born for but to be a Reformer, a Re-maker of what man has made, a renouncer of lies ; a restorer of truth and good, imitating that great Nature which embosoms us all, and which sleeps no moment on an old past, but every hour repairs itself, yielding us every morning a new day, and with every pulsation a new life ?

The guides of men must be Faith and Hope. " The Transcendentalist " describes what is meant by the term—the ends and aims of transcendentalism.

Thirdly, there are the Essays, twenty in number, the most remarkable of which, "History," illustrates his absurd exaggeration in exalting the importance of the individual as being the whole in epitome, and his contempt for concrete facts. "Self-Reliance " is one of his very best—"Trust yourself." " Compensation " is perhaps his soundest essay ; whilst " Spiritual Laws " is notable as containing one of his most beautiful passages.* " Prudence" and " Heroism " are well worth reading, the one illustrating his shrewd good sense, the other his nobility of character. " Over-

* Probably this passage : " A little consideration of what takes place around us every day would show us that a higher law than that of our will regulates events ; that our painful labours are unnecessary and fruitless ; that only in our easy, simple, spontaneous action are we strong, and by contenting ourselves with obedience we become divine. Belief and love—a believing love will relieve us of a vast load of care. O my brothers, God exists. There is a soul at the centre of nature, and over the will of every man. . . ."

Soul " illustrates his rhapsodical extravagance. In " Character " we have one of his best and most characteristic. " Manners " gives us a picture of the ideal gentleman. " Nature " is comprehensively characteristic on one side; " Politics," an excellent analysis of what ought to be meant by them.

Then come the lectures. Of those on " Representative Men "—*i.e.* Plato, the philosopher : Swedenborg, the mystic : Montaigne, the sceptic : Shakespeare, the poet : Napoleon, the Man of the World : Goethe, the writer : with the introductory lecture on the " Uses of Great Men "— it may be said that they are simply studies of the fictions of Emerson's own imagination, of the incarnations of Emersonian ideas, and it is not without impatience and irritation that any one who is conversant with the works of those great men can read these lectures, to say nothing of the introduction of such a person as Swedenborg into their company.

Next comes the collection of discourses ranged under the title of " The Conduct of Life." Among these we need not discriminate, and there is nothing to linger over.

Next comes the collection entitled " English Traits," the most concrete and popularly intelligible of Emerson's works.

And lastly come the poems, which will be dealt with later.

[The minimum for a student wishing to get an idea of Emerson would be a careful perusal of these pieces: "The Transcendentalist" (with which he should begin); "The American Scholar"; "The Address to the Divinity College Class"; "Self-Reliance"; "Man the Reformer"; "Character"; "Nature" (the essay, not the treatise); "Compensation"; "Spiritual Laws."]

Emerson is pre-eminently and essentially a transcendentalist. What is the meaning of the term ? He has himself explained it:

The Idealism of the present day acquired the name of Transcendental from the use of that term by Immanuel Kant, of Konigsberg, who replied to the sceptical philosophy of Locke, which insisted that there was nothing in the intellect which was not previously in the experience of the senses, by showing that there was a very important class of ideas or imperative forms which did not come by experience, but through which experience was acquired ; that these were intuitions of the mind itself ; and he denominated them *Transcendental* forms : whatever belongs to the class of intuitive thought is popularly called, at the present day, *Transcendental*.

He tells us himself that he preferred the terms "idealist" and "idealism," which he therefore employs. The idealist is the exact opposite of the materialist. The materialist takes his departure from the external world and esteems a man as one product of that world. The idealist takes his departure from his own consciousness and reckons the world an appearance. The materialist respects sensible masses, society, government, social art, and luxury, every establishment, every

mass, whether majority of numbers, or extent of
space, or amount of objects, every social action.
The idealist has another measure, which is metaphysical, namely, the rank which things themselves take in his consciousness. To him the only
reality is mind, of which men and all other
natures are better or worse reflectors. He is
himself the measure and the sum of all things.
To him the parts, particles, and varieties of
Nature and of man are One: he is a portion
of the Universal Spirit: the essence of genius, of
virtue, of life, of beauty, of goodness: the
supreme critic of the past, the sole prophet of the
future. His instincts are his guides; through
these instincts God speaks and has never ceased to
speak. Thus, as God is in him he is a law to
himself; he has only to surrender himself and be
loyally obedient to his instincts and he is God-like.
Man, therefore, has only to be true to himself and
to trust himself, and when in innocency or when
by intellectual perception he attains to say, " I
love the Right: Truth is beautiful within and
without for evermore. Virtue, I am thine, save
me, use me ; thee will I serve, day and night, in
great, in small, that I may be, not *virtuous*, but
virtue," then is the end of his being attained.
Thus in Emerson's philosophy the only faculty
which is of any avail is intuitive insight; the only
knowledge which avails is what intuitive insight
reveals and teaches. God, who spoke in the past,
is speaking in the present; God, who spoke to
Moses, to Socrates, to Jesus, speaks to every one
of us if we so rule our lives that we are fit to

receive His message. Revelation and God's gospel are the monopoly of no man and of no form of creed. Man is his own Church. If we obey perfectly the laws and conditions of our own being we have no need to model ourselves or regard with superstitious reverence any other man, whether Moses or Christ, whether Zoroaster or Socrates. Christ indeed was a noble example, inasmuch as he did what we as men may do.*

This will explain the enormous importance which he attaches to the individual man worked out in the essay on " Self-Reliance." As this immense importance attaches itself to the individual, the individual must know and feel the necessity for fitting himself for these responsibilities by proper culture. And on this culture—in other words, on what constitutes *education*—Emerson has much to say. And what he has to say is practically summed up in these pieces: " The American Scholar," " Culture," Behaviour, " " Manners." The end and aim of education are self-reliance and character. Its means are: First, the study of Nature, the realisation that Nature is the counterpart of man's soul, answering to it part for part; its beauty the beauty of the individual mind, its laws the laws of that mind. Secondly, the records of the Past, whether preserved in literature, art, or institutions, rationally, not superstitiously, studied. Thirdly, action and experience: " So much only of life as

* Read the remarkable passage in the Divinity Address at Cambridge July 15, 1838, beginning: " Jesus Christ belonged to the true race of prophets," etc.

I know by experience, so much of the wilderness
have I vanquished and planted, or so far have I
extended my being, my dominion." The least
important of these means is the second. And it
is here that Emerson reacts, and reacts extrava-
gantly, against the ordinary conception both of
the means and ends of education. To mere
book-learning he attaches scarcely any importance.

Meek young men [he contemptuously observes] grow up
in libraries believing it their duty to accept the views which
Cicero, which Locke, which Bacon have given; forgetful that
Cicero, Locke and Bacon were only young men in libraries when
they wrote those books.

Books are for nothing but to inspire. It is
absurd to make fetishes out of the literature of
the Past, for " each age, it is found, must write its
own books ; or rather each generation for the
next succeeding. The books of an older period
will not fit this." No, let us learn to walk on our
own feet, let us work with our own hands, let us
speak our own minds. " Books," he says, " are
for the scholar's idle times." Why should we
bow down before Plato or Shakespeare ? What is
immortal in them belongs to us : the Power which
inspired them inspires us. Great men appear
that greater men may succeed them.

There is one mind [he says in his essay on " History "] common
to all individual men. Every man is an inlet to the same and to
all of the same. What Plato has thought he may think ; what a
Saint has felt he may feel ; what at any time has befallen any
man he can understand. Who hath access to this universal mind
is a party to all that is or can be done, for this is the only and
sovereign agent.

Believing that man is essentially progressive and in process of creation, he has no superstitious reverence even for humanity's highest products.

What we once admired as poetry [he says in his lecture on "Poetry and Imagination"] has long since come to be a sound of tin-pans; and many of our later books we have outgrown. Perhaps Homer and Milton will be tin-pans yet.

If these are his views with regard to the demigods of his race it is not surprising that he looked down on mere learning, on scholarship, on the acquisition of facts and knowledge, on all that study and memory can acquire, with something very like contempt. His educational theory appears to proceed on the vast assumption that every youth is an Emerson, and to take no account at all of any youth who is not an Emerson. He quotes with approval the saying : " He that would bring home the wealth of the Indies must carry out the wealth of the Indies." He does not take into consideration the many who have not the wealth of the Indies, and the many who are quite content to bring home much less than the wealth of the Indies.

Now from all this it will be seen that we cannot go to Emerson for practical, methodical advice. He will supply us with wings, but he ignores the dead weight which those wings have to support ; he will furnish us with a balloon, but what he does not supply is an atmosphere to float it. We feel that as a practical teacher he is the architect of a noble fabric " pinnacled deep in the intense inane." He postulates the existence of

the results of education as the basis on which
education must rest. He disdains a knowledge of
grammar, of philology, of languages, as the mere
exercises of pedants; he disdains a knowledge of
the facts of history, and yet we are to be familiar
with the quintessence of what has been produced
by Homer and Plato, and by the great poets and
thinkers of all nations and of all ages, and expatiate
through the whole reel of the *philosophy* of
history. Indeed, Emerson stands in the same
relation to education in its practical aspects as
Ruskin stands to political economy as a branch of
science. In both transcendentalism is reduced to
an absurdity. But all this shows what all his
writings show, that we must go to Emerson, not
for practical, direct guidance, but for suggestion,
inspiration, impulse, leaving our common sense to
adjust the balance, and he becomes the more
helpful the nearer he approaches spiritual truth,
the truths discernible by spiritual insight. Take,
for example, the following, in which insight,
wisdom, and audacity go hand in hand:

The religion which is to guide and fulfil the present and
coming ages, whatever else it be, must be intellectual. The
scientific mind must have a faith which is science.

*   *   *   *   *   *

There will be a new church founded on moral science, at first
cold and naked, a babe in a manger again, the algebra and mathematics of ethical law, the church of men to come, without shawms,
or psaltery, or sackbut ; but it will have heaven and earth for its
beams and rafters : science for symbol illustration : it will fast
enough gather beauty, music, picture, poetry.*

----

* Essay on " Worship."

L

Again :

Hitch your waggon to a star. Let us not fag in paltry works which serve our pot and bag alone. Let us not lie and steal. No god will help. We shall find all their teams going the other way —Charles's Wain, Great Bear, Orion, Leo, Hercules : every god will leave us. Work rather for those interests which the divinities honour and promote — justice, love, freedom, knowledge, utility. *

Or take again his opinions on a subject on which, as certainty is impossible, consistency is impossible —the immortality of the soul in the sense of the protraction of the individual consciousness after physical dissolution :

I think all sound minds rest on a certain preliminary conviction, namely, that if it be best that conscious personal life shall continue, it will continue ; if not best, then it will not : and we, if we saw the whole, should of course see that it was better so.†

Again :

Everything is prospective, and man is to live hereafter. That the world is for his education is the only sane solution of the enigma.

But observe his honesty and consequent inconsistency. He must have known that, assuming the world is for man's education, and that everything is prospective, this is no argument for the immortality of individual man—for the race and type it may be, but not for the individual. And so in the same essay he writes :

I confess that everything connected with our personality fails. Nature never spares the individual ; we are always balked of a

---

* " Civilization."   † Essay on " Immortality."

complete success : no prosperity is promised to our self-esteem. We have our indemnity only in the moral and intellectual reality to which we aspire. That is immortal, and we only through that. The soul stipulates for no private good. That which is private I see not to be good. " If truth live, I live ; if justice live, I live," said one of the old saints, and these by any man's suffering are enlarged and enthroned.

There is just the same inconsistency, if inconsistency it really be, in Aristotle, in Shakespeare, in Goethe, and in Shelley. And when Emerson adds :

I am a better believer, and all serious souls are better believers, in the immortality than we can give grounds for. The real evidence is too subtle, or is higher than we can write down in propositions, and therefore Wordsworth's "Ode" is the best modern essay on the subject—

when he adds this, he not only indicates the reasons for such inconsistencies, but he assigns this question to its proper sphere : that empyreal region where reason, definition, logic, and every purely intellectual faculty alike fail us.

In his views on this great question we have in epitome, as it were, all that constitutes the great charm and power of Emerson as a seer, prophet, and teacher : his essential and pellucid honesty, his cheerful optimism, the dignity, serenity, and elevation of his temper, his complete emancipation from all the shackles of the senses and the carnal world, the faithfulness with which he strove to realise the aim of Plotinus, that is, to bring the God which is within man into harmony with the God which is in the universe : a beautiful soul, a beautiful example, a beautiful gospel.

We are naturally tempted to institute a comparison between him and his great friend Carlyle. In three great and fundamental points they were alike : both were tremendously in earnest, both were entirely and essentially honest, and both were transcendentalists. But for the rest the comparison lies in contrast. Emerson is an optimist, serene and unfaltering ; Carlyle a pessimist, fierce, turbulent, and perverse. To Carlyle the world was peopled mainly with fools and shams ; to Emerson the average man had in him the germs and potentialities of the demigods of our race. Carlyle was so diseased and wilful an egotist that though he preached duty and practised what he preached, he neither found any comfort or happiness in it himself, nor did he promise any comfort or happiness in it to any one else ; by Emerson's side stood Hope and Faith, transforming Duty and Labour into radiant happiness. Carlyle practically eliminates happiness as a factor in human energy—work, strive, endure, what have you to do with happiness ? " what if thou wert born and predestined not to be happy, but to be unhappy ? " With Emerson happiness in the true sense of the term is to be sought, to be cherished ; it is very sunlight to the soul. It is *always* to the dark side that Carlyle leans ; but instinctively as a plant makes for the light does Emerson make for the sun. As a preacher and commentator, Carlyle exhausts the vocabulary of intolerance, despair, and contempt ; nothing is so rare in Emerson as any indication of irritability, of intolerance, of sarcasm. Emerson too often misses his mark because he is so vague, so abstract, because he aims too high ; but Carlyle's blows have the precision and force of a blacksmith's hammer on his anvil. Carlyle's presentation and expression might be compared to meteoric flashes, lurid, wild, and grand; but we should not go to elementary forces for a simile to apply to presentation and expression in Emerson : rather we should go to a cabinet of gems, finely cut, coldly finished, most exquisitely polished. Into a comparison of the quality and tenor of their writings we need not enter.

As a poet Emerson cannot be said to hold a high place even among the poets of his country. He fails in some of the primary qualifications for producing really good poetry. His rhythm, particularly in the blank-verse poems, is often intolerably harsh and dislocated, and very seldom, even at its best, has it any charm : the utmost that can be said for it is that it is mechanically correct when it follows the conventional form. His grammar is often involved and his style cumbrous. Of evolution he has no sense : his poems are jerky, scrappy, and often exceedingly obscure. His poetry has no passion, little of the sensuous element, little simplicity : it has not the concreteness of effective poetry. So that Matthew Arnold has said—and who could be a better judge ?—that " The Bridge " of Longfellow or "The School of Days" of Whittier is of more poetic worth than all the verse of Emerson. His best poem so far as poetic quality and execution are

concerned is probably the hymn sung at the
completion of the Concord Monument, beginning :

> By the rude bridge that arched the flood,
> Their flag to April's breeze unfurl'd,
> Here once the embattled farmers stood,
> And fired the shot heard round the world.

Undoubtedly we do come across single stanzas and
passages which are excellent alike in conception
and expression, like :

> Though love repine, and reason chafe,
> There came a voice without reply :—
> " 'Tis man's perdition to be safe,
> When for the truth he ought to die." *

But if we take a criterion of poetry with which
Emerson has himself somewhat ambiguously
furnished us, " The great poets are judged by the
frame of mind they induce " †—if we take this,
then we must give him a higher place. For his
poetry is penetrated by the noble ideas which
pervade his prose. " It moves," as Oliver Wendell
Holmes truly says, " in a world of symbolism, the
sense of the infinite fills it with its majestic
presence." He is always seeing the universal in
the particular. It is pervaded with the spirit of
what Wordsworth indicated when he wrote :

> To me the meanest flower that blows can give
> Thoughts that do often lie too deep for tears ; ‡

---

* " Sacrifice."   † Preface to " Parnassus."
‡ " Ode to Immortality."

but this emotion with Emerson is spiritual, not æsthetic.

His most indulgent critic—I mean of critics entitled to serious consideration—O. W. Holmes, advises the reader of Emerson's poetry to begin with " The Problem " and go on to " Each and All," " The Humble Bee," " The Snowstorm," " Monadnoc," and after this " Wood-Notes." He also greatly admires the paragraph in " May Day " beginning :

> I saw the bud-crowned Spring go forth.

But above all he draws attention to the beauty of the " Threnody "—the poem written by Emerson on his son's death—though when he places it beside the finest memorial poems in our language, I think many of us can only listen in respectful amazement, and be *confirmed* in what on the face of it seemed probable, that Matthew Arnold is a more trustworthy critic of Emerson's poetry than Oliver Wendell Holmes.

Emerson, like all men of true genius, took his own measure. He is not a great writer, he is not a great philosopher; he lacks concentration, architecture, symmetry, unity :

> Expect nothing more of my power of construction [he said]— no ship-building, no clipper smack, nor skiff even, only boards and thongs tied together.

Again, he says :

> Here I sit and read with very little system, and as far as regards composition with the most fragmentary result : paragraphs incom pressible, each sentence an infinitely repellent particle.

He has left us no sustained composition, no regularly evolved thesis or essay. His sentences and paragraphs resemble mosaic work, or perhaps his essays and lectures may be compared to cabinets of gems—gems generally brilliant, often of the first water, always exquisitely polished, but unstrung and unset. He himself speaks of his " lapidary " style. He is not only a plagiarist in the sense of appropriating the thoughts, the sentiments, and the phrases of other writers, but he glories in the plagiarism. He says of Plutarch :

> In his immense quotation and allusion we quickly cease to discriminate between what he quotes and what he invents. We sail on his memory into the ports of every nation, enter into every private property, and do not stop to discriminate owners, but give him the praise of all.

And this is exactly true of himself. But what he borrowed he made his own by its collocation, its purpose, its application. He treated books as he treated Nature, he Emersonised both. As a master of style and composition he must be judged not by the total impression of any given piece, but by its sentences and paragraphs : he must be judged by fragments. And with the composition of these he took immense pains. He is a master of epigram, terse, lucid, incisive ; but he aims too much at dazzling and surprising, and not always legitimately and in good taste, and so he is sometimes cheaply " smart," and even flippant, resorting to paradox, forced antitheses, affected quaintness, and the grossest exaggeration. But at his best he is really eloquent, clothing his conceptions worthily and nobly. His sketches from Nature are often masterpieces of poetic prose—in rhythm exquisitely musical, in diction most felicitous. His style has always the mark of distinction, but it is not the distinction of the great classics of prose : he has not their power of evolution, of combination, of subduing their material to literary expression in its most effectively appropriate forms.

Emerson then is not a classic as a literary artist either in verse or in prose, and so we come round to what we started with. We are in the presence of a seer, of a prophet, of the preacher of a most inspiring gospel. He cannot better be summed up than in the words of Oliver Wendell Holmes, who fancifully represents Emerson as starting on life the recipient of certain sealed orders which, when he was about thirty years of age, he was to open and read. They ran :

Thou shalt not profess that which thou dost not believe.

Thou shalt not heed the voice of man when it agrees not with the voice of God in thine own soul.

Thou shalt study and obey the laws of the universe, and they will be thy fellow-servants.

Thou shalt speak the truth as thou seest it, without fear, in the spirit of kindness to all thy fellow-creatures, dealing with the manifold interests of life and the typical characters of history.

Nature shall be to thee as a symbol. The life of the soul, in conscious union with the Infinite, shall be for thee the only real existence.

This pleasing show of an external world through which thou art passing is given thee to interpret by the light which is in thee. Its least appearance is not unworthy of thy study. Let thy soul be open and thine eyes will reveal to thee beauty everywhere.

Go forth with thy message among thy fellow-creatures ; teach them that they must trust themselves as guided by that inner light which dwells with the pure in heart, to whom it was promised of old that they shall see God.

Teach them that each generation begins the world afresh in perfect freedom : that the present is not the prisoner of the past, but that to-day holds captive all yesterdays, to compare, to judge, to accept, to reject their teachings, as these are shown by its own morning's sun.

To thy fellow-countrymen thou shalt preach the gospel of the New World, that here, in our America, is the home of man, that here is the promise of a new and more excellent social state than history has recorded.

Thy life shall be as thy teachings, brave, pure, truthful, beneficent, hopeful, cheerful, hospitable to all honest belief, all sincere thinkers, and active according to thy gifts and opportunities.*

Such were Emerson's "sealed orders," and he obeyed them to the letter, and because he obeyed them so loyally and so fearlessly he is and will long be a power, and a great power, among the young and impressionable : he will contribute much to mould those powers which, in their maturity, mould the world.

* From O. W. Holmes' "Ralph Waldo Emerson." The extract is given by kind permission of Messrs. Kegan Paul, Trench, Trübner and Co.

MATTHEW ARNOLD

IN striking contrast to the Transcendentalist whose career and work we have been considering stands Matthew Arnold. Here all is balance, sobriety, and measure: here refined good sense, precision, lucidity: all that a temper and genius finely touched, delicate, sensitive, pure, nourished and inspired by intimate, habitual, and most sympathetic communion with what is excellent and classical in the leading and master literatures of the world: all that such a temper and genius thus educated and disciplined might be expected to achieve. But in character, to employ the word in the Emersonian sense, strangely and signally deficient, having the power to charm but not to impress and inspire, appealing rather to what is implied in " taste " than to what is implied in " soul." As a critic, exquisite and within certain consummate limits unrivalled among his countrymen; as a satirist, quite delicious and worthy to stand as a master of irony beside the author of the *Lettres Provinciales;* as a poet, in poetic quality as well as in fascinating felicity of expression second only among his contemporaries to Tennyson. But he aspired to be a Reformer and Teacher. He waged a lifelong war against Philistinism, the curse of our nation—that quality which he himself defined as " on the side of beauty and taste, vulgarity; on the side of morals and feeling, coarseness; on the side of mind and spirit, unintelligence." * But here he failed in character; he was not made of the stuff out of which Reformers are made. He had no enthusiasm: nothing of the magnetism which intensity of conviction and intensity of purpose inspire: he was timid, sensitive, and self-conscious, afraid of ridicule, and especially of the ridicule which earnestness and emphasis so easily excite in "superior people." He was not one of those who can lose themselves to find themselves. Perhaps the nearest analogy to him among Reformers is Erasmus. Like Erasmus, he had no taste for martyrdom, for leading desperate charges or forlorn hopes. Like Erasmus, he was deficient in moral courage. Like Erasmus, he fought with weapons too light and finely tempered to make any impression on his pachydermatous adversaries. And when he entered the arena of theological controversy and pleaded against the Orthodox party for the re-interpretation and reconstruction of Christianity he failed equally. He carried little weight and no authority, partly for the same reasons that he failed as an anti-Philistine, but partly, and here perhaps mainly, for another reason: he had not the requisite credentials. In the conflict with Philistinism no one could question his right to speak with authority on all that pertained to Belles Lettres. But in theology he was no scholar, and its pundits remained contemptuously indifferent to

* Introduction to "Celtic Literature."

an adversary who knew nothing of Hebrew, nothing of the Oriental languages, little of patristic literature, little of the vast literature which has gathered round the subject in modern times, and whose knowledge was somewhat superficial. And here he made many grave mistakes, mistakes arising not merely from insufficiency of learning and information, but mistakes of temper. At his best Matthew Arnold may be regarded as the crown and flower of our old academic culture. Newdigate Prizeman, Fellow of Oriel, Professor of Poetry, his genius took its ply and colour from academic society and associations when that society was, in the Oxford of 1843, at the acme of its potentiality and accomplishment, when the common room at Oriel was in its glory, when Newman was preaching at St. Mary's, and Church, and Stanley, and Clough, and Froude, and Jowett were as Arnold's coevals or seniors, all busy and all influential in their several spheres: when Oxford was still aristocratic and conservative, still, in Arnold's own words, whispering the last enchantments of the middle age, still true to the ideal, still true to the beautiful: still standing four-square to the aggressions and menaces of the democracy, the Philistines, and *Das Gemeine*. It has all gone now for good or evil—some of us think for evil— that Oxford of Arnold's youth and apprenticeship. It produced a type of men which is now all but obsolete, and which will soon be as extinct as the dodo or the ichthyosaurus—the type which gave us the " Scholar-Gipsy " and " Thyrsis " and the

" Essays in Criticism" and " Friendship's Garland " and " Ionica." As Dante summed up in the most comprehensive sense the Middle Ages, as well on the side of achievement as of limitation, so Matthew Arnold may be said as comprehensively to sum up, in his character and in his writings, Academic Oxford at its acme, not in its relation to learning, but in its relation to life.

His life was singularly uneventful. Born at Laleham, near Staines, on Christmas Eve 1822, he was the eldest son of Thomas Arnold, afterwards the famous head-master of Rugby, and Mary his wife, who was a Miss Penrose, belonging to a most scholarly family and a woman of distinguished intellect and character. At thirteen and a half years of age he was sent to Winchester School, then under a most accomplished classical scholar, Dr. Moberly, afterwards Bishop of Salisbury; but after remaining at Winchester for about a year he was removed to Rugby that he might be under the surveillance of his father. At Rugby, Clough, the poet, and Thomas Hughes, the author of " Tom Brown's Schooldays," were his schoolfellows. In 1840 he gained the Balliol Scholarship and went into residence at Balliol in 1841. After winning the Newdigate Prize Poem on Cromwell in 1843 and obtaining a second class in the Literæ Humaniores School—for which, had his father been alive, he would probably have been sternly rebuked—he was elected Fellow of Oriel—then a very great honour—in 1845. For a time he returned to Rugby as an assistant master under Dr. Tait, teaching classics to the fifth form; but in 1847 he was made private secretary to Lord Lansdowne, then President of the Council. In 1849, in his twenty-seventh year, he published his first volume of poems, "The Strayed Reveller, and other Poems," by A., which fell still-born from the press. On April 14, 1851, began his long connection with education—the official business of five-and-thirty years of his life—for in that year he was appointed one of the Inspectors of Schools. The drudgery involved in this office must have been very galling and irksome to him, and indeed it reminds us of Schiller's *jeu d'esprit* "Pegasus in Harness," to see the poet of "Thyrsis" and the "Scholar-Gipsy" dragging in such a yoke. But he was neither recalcitrant nor complaining. He was not, as Sir Joshua Fitch once sighed to me, an ideal school inspector and all that the fancy of his official superiors and coadjutors could paint, but he was a more conscientious drudge than Caliban. And in the higher and more ornamental departments of his calling he did splendid services to education, as is proved by his work as Foreign Assistant Commissioner on Education to visit France, Holland, Belgium, Switzerland, and Piedmont, in 1859, embodied in a Parliamentary Blue Book published afterwards, in 1861, as "Popular Education in France, with Notices of Holland and Switzerland"; by his services as a Critic of the Revised Code of 1862; by his Report upon Schools and Universities on the Continent; and by his Report on the Education of Germany published in 1874.

Just after the initiation of his official life he made a very happy marriage, and if the burden of much which life entailed on him was heavy, it was lightened by being shared. In 1852 appeared "Empedocles on Etna, and other Poems," by A. Again the poems fell quite flat, though this volume contained some of the best things he ever wrote. In 1855 appeared a second series of Poems, this time under his own name. In 1857 he was elected Professor of Poetry at Oxford, an office which he held for a double term of ten years. As Professor of Poetry he produced much of his best critical work, initiated in 1858 by his drama of "Merope," with its elaborate preface justifying classicism. This was followed in 1861 by his three lectures "On Translating Homer," supplemented in the following year by a fourth. These are among his most valuable critical essays. In 1865 appeared what is probably his masterpiece in criticism and in style, the "Essays in Criticism." His last lectures as Professor of Poetry were the four on Celtic Literature, published in 1867; this is perhaps Matthew Arnold's most comprehensively representative work in criticism as well on the side of limitation and defect as on the side of excellence. The same year saw the appearance of "New Poems," which, with much which did not add to his reputation, contained also one of the most exquisite of his poems, and perhaps his masterpiece, the memorial verses on Clough entitled "Thyrsis."

In 1869 appeared the manifesto, his first serious and systematic attack on Philistinism and plea for sweetness and light, in "Culture and Anarchy," a series of essays reprinted from the *Cornhill*; while between 1866 and 1870 he was running a series of letters through the *Pall Mall Gazette* dealing chiefly with the Franco-Prussian War, afterwards republished as "Friendship's Garland."

In 1870 his theological works began with "St. Paul and Protestantism," in which he may be said to have broken with Orthodoxy: this was succeeded in 1873 by "Literature and Dogma," in which he was even more outspoken, protesting against the anthropomorphic idea of God and reliance on miracles as supports of Christianity, and sometimes in a spirit of levity which, to say the least, was exceedingly unbecoming. Two years afterwards in "God and the Bible," a series of essays reprinted from the *Contemporary Review*, he gave what was at once a sequel to the former work and a reply to its critics. With his "Last Essays on Church and State" his theological writings closed. Over his contributions to current politics we need not linger. The best, the only permanently valuable work of his last days, as indeed of his whole life, belongs to literary criticism, to essays scattered through what he calls the "Mixed Essays" and to what is included in the posthumous volume, the second series of "Essays in Criticism," and in what is included in the "American Discourses." He died with appalling suddenness at Liverpool, April 15, 1888.

When we say that Matthew Arnold had his full share of sharp and bitter domestic sorrow in the

M

loss of loved children, that his services as a public servant met with the most niggard recognition, and that in his application for posts which might have relieved him from repulsive drudgery and given him leisure for more congenial pursuits he was always disappointed; that during the greater part of his life he had neither fame nor authority nor influence, filling a subordinate position, and, if not actually poor, always grazing embarrassment; that his literary work was not easy to him, but that it was the result of very severe labour; that he felt and acknowledged that he had not been what men call a success in life, though he would gladly have shared life's honours, rewards, and vantage-grounds, for he was neither an enthusiast nor recluse, but quite a man of the world and of society, or at least affected to be such; yet, for all this, he was never other than cheerful, genial, playful, and uncomplaining, the most delightful of companions, the most affectionate of husbands, of fathers, and of friends. A single sentence in one of his letters is so significant both of his position and of his temper that it may be quoted. Writing to Mr. John (now Lord) Morley, he says:

I announced yesterday at the office my intention of retiring. Gladstone will never promote the author of "Literature and Dogma" if he can help it, and meanwhile my life is drawing to an end, and I have no wish to execute the Dance of Death in an elementary school.

It was indeed, sufficiently disgraceful to England that he should have had to execute some of the most beautiful poems and some of the most

precious critical essays in our language, as he
actually did, in elementary schools.

But this is only very partially the Arnold who
concerns us; this is the Arnold who is lying in
Laleham Churchyard. The Arnold who concerns
us is the Arnold of the *personality* impressed on his
writings, and more especially on his poetry.

As a prose writer Matthew Arnold comes before
us in four distinct capacities : as a critic of modern
life and society, as a critic of literature, as a critic
and reconstructor of popular theology, as a critic
of the theory and practice of education. An
account of his work in relation to education will
not come within the scope of this essay, but those
who are interested in it may consult with advantage Sir Joshua Fitch's monograph on the
Arnolds in the series on Great Educators,
published by Mr. Heinemann.

I shall not so much criticise as interpret
Matthew Arnold's attitude, tenets, and opinions ;
and therefore, with as little critical commentary
as possible, I propose to review his chief writings
in each of the divisions under which those writings
may be arranged.

In dealing with modern life and society he was,
as we shall see, more successful as a critic and
satirist than as a reformer, or even as one who
contributed in any way directly to reform. " It
is not in my nature," he said of himself, " to
dispute on behalf of any opinion, even my own,
very obstinately." Hence he never inspired
enthusiasm, he never even succeeded in creating

the impression that he was in earnest. An incomparable master of persiflage and irony, the rival of Lord Beaconsfield as a coiner of delicately felicitous phrases and turns of sarcasm, most urbane when most irritating, most pleasant when most caustic, he seemed to revel in season and out of season in the display of these accomplishments. A reformer who begins by resolving his reformees into Barbarians, Philistines, and Populace—each analysed into caricatures which are masterpieces of satire and ridicule—and then in the way of admonishment and advice assumes toward them the attitude assumed by Shakespeare's Touchstone towards Corin and Audrey, is hardly likely to further the cause of reform. And this was too often Matthew Arnold's attitude and method. And therefore he carried little weight in the conflict in which he engaged. He failed in impressiveness and authority. And a reformer who fails in these qualities is pretty sure to fail in his object.

The main object and purport of "Culture and Anarchy," which appeared in 1869, is described by himself :

The whole scope of the essay is to recommend culture as the great help out of our present difficulties : culture being a pursuit of our total perfection by means of getting to know, on all matters which most concern us, the best which has been thought and said in the world ; and through this knowledge, turning a stream of fresh and free thought upon our stock notions and habits, which we now follow staunchly but mechanically, vainly imagining that there is a virtue in following them staunchly which makes up for the mischief of following them mechanically.*

---

* Preface.

It will be seen that the most importantly significant words here are " our present difficulties "—Matthew Arnold's urbane expression for what he will presently analyse in a very irritating manner ; our " stock notions and habits," which he will submit to a similar analysis ; and, lastly, what he means by " culture."

" Our present difficulties " are the predominance of such ideas as Bright's, who believed that " the people of the United States have offered to the world more valuable information during the last forty years than all Europe put together," and who had defined culture as " a smattering of the two dead languages of Greek and Latin " ; the predominance of an impression that England is great and admirable because of its machinery, because every one can say what he pleases, because we can do as we like, because of our coal-supply, our wealth, our population, and our good health ; in other words, the predominance of the doctrines preached by such men as Roebuck, Odger, Bradlaugh, Hepworth Dixon, Robert Buchanan, and other Radicals, Nonconformists, and Agnostics, and roared out each morning to an approving and admiring nation by the "young lions of the *Daily Telegraph*." If to these be added the ingrained Philistinism of the typical Englishman— " on the side of beauty and taste, vulgarity ; on the side of morals and feeling, coarseness; on the side of mind and spirit, unintelligence "—and the fact that in a country the very breath of whose being is freedom there are no bodies, no institutions, no sort of organisation of sufficient weight and authority to counteract this anarchy: if we remember this, we shall have no difficulty in understanding the origin of what he calls " our present difficulties." With regard to our " stock notions and habits," they may be deduced from the causes, for their predominance constitutes the causes of " our present difficulties." The remedy lies in " culture," and " the great men of culture are those who have had a passion for diffusing, for making prevail, for carrying from one end of society to the other, the best knowledge, the best ideas of a given time ; who have laboured to divest knowledge of all that was harsh, uncouth, difficult, abstract, professional, exclusive ; to humanise it, to make it efficient outside the clique of the cultivated and learned, yet still remaining the best knowledge and thought of the time, and a true source, therefore, of sweetness and light " ; and culture in itself is " a study of perfection," the harmonious expansion of *all* the powers which make the beauty and worth of human nature : it is what the Greeks called εὐφυΐα, the possession of a finely tempered nature—a harmonious perfection, a perfection in which the characters of beauty and intelligence are both present, which unites, as Swift calls them, the two noblest of things, sweetness and light.

In analysing English society, as he does in the third chapter, into *Barbarians* (*i.e.* the aristocracy, Tennyson's " broad-shouldered genial Englishman "), Philistines (the average members of the middle classes), the Populace (the British workman and the patrons and admirers of such prints as the *British Banner*), he shows how deplorably deficient all are in the remotest appreciation of such ideals as culture implies, how ugly, how dismal, how cheerless their lives. Look, he says, at the life of the aristocracy, with their culture all external; their gifts and graces in looks, manners, accomplishments, prowess; their field sports, their capabilities and potentialities as compared with what they are. "Look at the life, imaged in such a paper as the *Nonconformist*—a life of jealousy of the Establishment, disputes, tea meetings, openings of chapels, sermons." * Look at the suicide of a Mr. Smith, secretary to some insurance company, who, it was said, "laboured under the impression that he would come to poverty, and that he was eternally lost." †

In a most interesting chapter—chap. iv.—he analyses the characteristics of the two great powers in culture and moral influence, *Hebraism* and *Hellenism*. The essentials of the first he sums up admirably in the preface:

To walk staunchly by the best light one has, to be strict and sincere with oneself, not to be of the number of those who say and do not, to be in earnest—this is the discipline by which alone man is enabled to rescue his life from thraldom to the passing moment and to his bodily senses, to ennoble it and to make it eternal. And this discipline has been nowhere so effectively taught as in the school of Hebraism.

But it is time, he says, to Hellenise and to praise *knowing*, for we have Hebraised too much

* "Sweetness and Light."
† "Porro Unum est Necessarium."

and have overvalued doing. And what is Hellenising? Striving to see things in their true nature and as they really are; insisting on perfection, not on one side of our nature, but on all sides; cultivating a "full harmonious development of our humanity," a free play of thought upon our routine notions, "spontaneity of consciousness," sweetness and light; understanding what is implied in the true saying that "no man who knows nothing else, knows even his Bible"; acquiring measure, balance, symmetry; avoiding fanaticism and extravagance, through the attainment of ἐπιείκεια, sweet reasonableness, the being possessed by a disinterested desire to converse with what is excellent and beautiful, with what expands, elevates, and refines our nature. This is Hellenising, this is culture, and when we have learned to temper with this the Hebraising which we have too exclusively cultivated and admired, then we may hope that if any of us have the misfortune to commit suicide it will not be for the reasons that impelled poor Mr. Smith to take that unfortunate step, then we may hope that Philistinism will at least cease to be influential.

Men seldom respect those who amuse them, and are never docile when irritated, and as "Culture and Anarchy" had both these effects, it made very little serious impression on Arnold's contemporaries. Now, however, we see how much wisdom underlay its persiflage and satire, and can only regret that what it pleads for and suggests should have had so little effect on those who regulate our systems of higher education.

" Culture and Anarchy " was succeeded in the following year by " St. Paul and Protestantism," which is in a sense supplementary to " Culture and Anarchy." It is the application of the culture for which he pleaded, and in which alone he saw salvation, to dogmatic theology. In speaking of Hebraism he had especially identified it with Puritanism, in which he found its completest and most emphatic expression. Renan, in his work on St. Paul, had summed up his review of the great Apostle's life and teachings by observing that Paul is now coming to the end of his reign. Throughout his work Renan had associated St. Paul indissolubly with Protestantism, and as he had a strong distaste for Protestantism, it was with much satisfaction that he could pronounce that Paul was coming to the end of his reign. Matthew Arnold entered the arena in defence of St. Paul, contending that what was coming to the end of its reign was the form of Protestantism which had abused and misrepresented St. Paul, not St. Paul himself, who was, on the contrary, the most influential and vital force in true Christianity. The great object of the work was to dissociate the Apostle from the Puritanism which had claimed him for its great pundit. And this Arnold does by maintaining that the three essential terms of Pauline theology are not as popular theology makes them, namely, *calling, justification, sanctification,* but " dying with Christ," " resurrection from the dead," " growing into Christ," and these terms he rationalises by insisting that they should be understood in a symbolic sense, though he admits that St. Paul accepted the physical miracle of Christ's resurrection and ascension as a part of the signs and wonders which accompanied Christianity. But it is not within the scope of this essay to discuss the contentions of this most unsatisfactory book, which, while it revolted the Orthodox, pleased no one. Wholly devoid of any, even of literary, charm, without unction, without humour—a quality which is not perhaps to be expected on such a subject—its attraction lies partly in its pathos, and partly because it introduces an important group of Arnold's writings : I use the word "pathos" because of the sympathy which most people would feel with any one who should spring to arms in defence of the author of the Epistles to the Romans and the Corinthians. Still, we feel it would have been better to have let St. Paul alone. We cannot deal with him as we deal with Plato. We know, we *feel* that he would have repudiated his champion : the Puritans understood him much better than Arnold. It is not fair and honest to resolve into mere symbol what to St. Paul was most certainly not symbol, but fact. St. Paul was not a poet.

The next work, "Literature and Dogma," applies to Christianity generally the same methods and the same aims. It is in effect addressed, as "God and the Bible" was afterwards,

not to the man still striving to be content with the received theology. . . . Neither is it intended for a frivolous upper class in their religious insensibility, nor for a raw lower class in their religious insensibility, nor for Liberal secularists at home or abroad, nor for Catholics who are strangers, or very nearly so, to the Bible. . . . It is meant for those who, won by the modern spirit to habits of intellectual seriousness, cannot receive what sets these habits at nought, and will not try to force themselves to do so.*

Arnold proposes to throw over every theological dogma based on supernaturalism, and to resolve God into the manifestation of " an Eternal Power not ourselves making for Righteousness and Perfection." We are to regard all those texts and portions of Scripture on which the teachings of what is called Orthodox Christianity are based as either symbolic or irrelevant, and set stead only on those—and a strange jumble of Old and New Testament he makes in selecting them—which have spiritual significance, such as " Trust in God "—but he would prefer to substitute for " God " " the Eternal "—" Righteousness tendeth to life ! " " As the whirlwind passeth, so is the wicked no more, but the righteous is an everlasting foundation," † " Learn of me that I am mild and lowly in heart, and ye shall find rest unto your souls," ‡ " To him that ordereth his conversation right shall be shown the salvation of God," § and the like. Christianity is *the* Revelation, because Jesus Christ came to reveal what righteousness

* Preface to " God and the Bible." This quotation and such others as are still protected by copyright have been retained in this essay by kind permission of Messrs. Macmillan and Co.

† Proverbs x. 25.   ‡ Matt. xi. 39.

§ Psalm l. 23. The quotations are as given in " Culture and Anarchy."

really is, to show that nothing will do except righteousness, and that no other conception of righteousness will do except Jesus Christ's conception of it—His method, His secret, and His temper : His *method* being " the setting up a great unceasing inward movement of attention and verification in matters which are three-fourths of human life, where to see true and to verify is not difficult, the difficult thing is to *care* and to *attend* " ; His *secret* being spiritual insight, the discovery of the new man which, after God, is created in righteousness and true holiness ; His *temper* being His sweet reasonableness, the fulness in Him of humility, grace, and truth.

It is not to be denied that in this most unsatisfactory book there is much which is helpful and beautiful and eloquent. Perhaps the best criticism of it would be what one Dr. Cuffe said of Bacon's *Novum Organum*, that " a foolish man could not, and a wise man would not, have written it." It certainly does not appeal to logic, for if the supernatural elements in Christianity are fictions and fables, no other conclusion can be drawn than that those who reported them were either impostors or deluded fanatics, and therefore as untrustworthy in what *Eclecticism* accepts from them as in what it rejects. It could scarcely fail to offend and irritate—for it is disfigured by many passages more than bordering on flippancy—many hundreds at least as intelligent and cultivated as its author ; and, lastly, it was somewhat premature. What has grown up historically can only dissolve historically, and

Arnold served the cause he had at heart much more effectually in pleading the cause of general culture. Religion is the poetry of morality: it neither springs from the reason nor does it appeal to the reason; its seat is in the imagination, the affections, and the conscience; and if it is to be modified, it is through *their* education that that modification must be effected. It is in forgetting this that the great mistake of the author of such a work as " Literature and Dogma " lies. Education must *precede* the work of demolition and reconstruction—the education of the *Zeitgeist*. All demolition, perhaps all reform, before this must be premature.

" Literature and Dogma " was immediately succeeded by " God and the Bible," which is partly a reply to those who had objected to the former work, and partly an expansion of it. Again the key is in the preface:

At the present moment two things about the Christian religion must surely be clear to anybody with eyes in his head. One is that men cannot do without it; the other that they cannot do with it as it is.

Again he essays to show " the truth and necessity of Christianity, and also its charm for the heart, mind, and imagination of man, even though the supernatural, which is now its popular sanction, should have to be given up." He defends it against the rabid hostility of Professor Clifford, who had called it " that awful plague which has destroyed two civilisations," and against such grotesquely anthropomorphic conceptions of it as found expression in the sermons of Moody—of Moody and Sankey fame. In two chapters he deals with the question of the " personality of God," demolishing in the first the God of miracles, in the second the God of metaphysics ; in the third dealing with the God of experience—all very polemical and wearisome, and to any one with a sense of humour most indecently grotesque. In a fourth chapter, " The Bible-Canon," he defends what he had said about the insufficiency of the record on which what we know of Jesus rests. The last two chapters are occupied with an elaborate dissertation on the Fourth Gospel, written with the object of showing that the Fourth Gospel was not written by St. John, and that though St. John is not responsible for some of the sayings attributed to our Lord, he was the chief source of most of them.

It is with far more satisfaction that we turn to Matthew Arnold as a literary critic : here he was at his best and could speak with an authority which none could dispute. It is by this work and by his poetry that he will live, but larger deductions perhaps must be made from the value of his work as a critic than from the value of his work as a poet.

Matthew Arnold's master and model in criticism, as he owned and repeatedly averred, was Sainte-Beuve, who occupies a rare, a most distinguished, a unique place in the history of criticism. In Arnold we English might have had our Sainte-Beuve, and that he does not fill a place in our own literature corresponding to the place filled by Sainte-Beuve in French literature is one of the greatest misfortunes which have befallen English letters. But unhappily the necessity for earning a livelihood in his professional calling, the labour and time expended on his official reports on educational questions, and, above all, the dissipation of his energy in his various contributions to theology, social questions, and politics, effectually prevented this. In such a life concentration was impossible : the varied extensive catholic learning and knowledge requisite for the equipment of a great critic he had no time to acquire, nor had he leisure to digest and meditate. So that all his work was more or less occasional and fragmentary, and some of it very superficial, and to himself, as he often said, most unsatisfactory. Sainte-Beuve dedicated his whole life, his whole energy, to literary criticism, to preparation, to production : when in the maturity of his powers and of his attainments the composition of one of the *Causeries du Lundi* occupied him exactly the whole of six days every week. " I never," he wrote, " have a holiday. On Monday towards noon I lift up my head and breathe for about an hour : after that the wicket shuts again and I am in my prison cell for seven days," and he is represented by upwards of forty volumes octavo. Two volumes would easily contain all that Matthew Arnold has left as a critic.

Before discussing his indebtedness to Sainte-Beuve and his general characteristics as a critic, let me briefly review his chief critical essays. First would come the preface to the Poems of 1853, in which he explains why he excluded " Empedocles on Etna " from the poems which he wished to preserve, and in which he discusses the materials proper for sound poetry and the characteristics of " the grand style." Then the preface to " Merope," in which he explains and justifies the canons of Greek tragedy, and pleads the cause of Classicism as opposed to Romanticism. Next comes one of his chief and most characteristic works—indeed, his masterpiece in criticism—viz. the " Essays in Criticism," published in 1865, and which may be regarded as the connecting link between his writings dealing with social criticism and those dealing with literary subjects. We may note especially its inimitable preface; its admirable chapters on the Function of Criticism at the present time and Literary Influence of Academies; the sympathetic insight which distinguishes the almost epoch-marking critiques on Heine, on Joubert, and on Marcus Aurelius ; the finely discriminating perception of the essential differences between pagan and religious sentiment displayed in the essay on that subject. Next would come the lectures " On Translating Homer," with their masterly analysis of the essential attributes of the genius which gave us the " Iliad " and the " Odyssey," and the light thrown on the true principles of translation. Next come the lectures on the study of Celtic literature, the most brilliant, the least satisfactory of all his critical writings—the least

satisfactory because, without having any pretension to being a Celtic scholar, without, in fact,
being able to construe a sentence of the original
languages, he generalised not only on the spirit
and tone, but on the style of the Celtic writers ;
because, having no critical knowledge of Celtic
literature, he hopelessly jumbled up what was
genuine and spurious, what was ancient and
modern, and sometimes attributed exclusively to
the Celts what were not their exclusively peculiar
characteristics : the most brilliant because, speaking generally and broadly, he did bring out some
of the differentiating characteristics of the three
racial elements which enter into the British
constitution, temper, and genius, and consequently into the English literature ; and because
the lectures are full of the finest critical insight, full
of precious suggestioning, full of rare and sound
instruction, exquisitely felicitous in expression,
masterpieces of style. Among his miscellaneous
critical essays prominence must be given to the
Introduction to Mr. Humphry Ward's " British
Poets," which, being a review of the history and
evolution of British poetry, is the most comprehensive of his critical essays ; to his review of
Mr. Stopford Brooke's Primer, with its somewhat
inadequate appreciation of Shakespeare, who is
called to account on the score of style and
deficiency as an artist ; to his essay on " A French
Critic on Milton," with its strange insensibility
to the moral greatness of the mighty Puritan ;
to the essay on Shelley, in which surely justice is
not done in very important respects to Shelley's

N

genius and work. In the admirable essay on
Wordsworth we are surprised at the critic's
indifference to Wordsworth's philosophy and
philosophical poems ; in the essays on Gray,
on Keats, on Byron, slight as they are, we see
Arnold at his very best.

Sainte-Beuve, as we have seen, was Arnold's
master and model as a critic. Let us see how.
In the memoir which Matthew Arnold wrote of
his master in the " Encyclopædia Britannica " he
says of him when he began his work as a critic :

> Something of fervour, enthusiasm, poetry he may have lost,
> but he had become a perfect critic—a critic of measure, not
> exuberant ; of the centre, not provincial ; of keen industry and
> curiosity, with " Truth " (the word engraved in English on his
> seal) for his motto ; moreover, with gay and amiable temper, his
> manner as good as his matter—the *critique souriant*, as in Charles
> Monselet's dedication to him he is called.

To become such a critic was Matthew Arnold's
aim. As we have already seen, Nature and
education must have so tempered him, so led
him instinctively to that ideal, long before he
came into contact with Sainte-Beuve's writings,
that he must have met the influence of his master
more than half-way. We have seen how essentially
Greek he was : how penetrated with the influence
of Greek ; how attracted to what was in the true
sense " classical " in Greek, in Latin, in French,
in German, in English — balance, measure,
sobriety, " form " — revolted by what was
amorphous, extravagant, coarse, with a genius
delicate and finely touched rather than robust
and vigorous, with a tendency to reduce and

submit everything to the standards and touch-stones of a lucid intelligence. Now it is doing the French—and Sainte-Beuve was pre-eminently and essentially a Frenchman—no injustice to say that though on such qualities and on such a temper is based the diathesis of a consummate critic, yet that critic will have his limitations, and they will be serious. Consummate he may be, but it will be within a certain sphere. The moment he is confronted, say, with such rude, crude, elemental forces as Walt Whitman, or such flights as Shakespeare's in " Lear," nay, with what is most characteristic of the Hebrew Prophets, of Pindar, even of our own Milton, his touchstones and standards are apt to fail him. And this is strikingly true of Sainte-Beuve. It would certainly be too hard on him to say unreservedly that his insight and success as a critic are in an inverse ratio to the greatness of the subjects and authors whom he judges, but it is assuredly in a certain degree true. Virgil he can measure and understand, but not Pindar ; Sophocles, but not Æschylus ; Cowper, but not Milton. There was much, and very much, revealed to Hazlitt and Lamb, who were most certainly not of the centre, which was not revealed to Sainte-Beuve and Matthew Arnold. It is a provoking and perplexing truth in relation to criticism that none but an enthusiast can under-stand an enthusiast, and of all critics an enthusiast is the worst. Matthew Arnold's range of sym-pathy and insight was wider than Sainte-Beuve's, but we cannot but feel that, in somewhat timid deference to his master, he deliberately confined them.

But how great, how salutary were his services to criticism. He taught it measure, sobriety, lucidity, precision. He derived his canons from the habitual, discriminating, and sympathetic study of all that was most excellent in the literature of ancient Greece and Rome, of modern Italy, of England, of France, of Germany. He may from constitution and temper have been limited in some of the directions indicated, but he was all but infallible in what he actually pronounced. His judgment was a very Ithuriel's spear in the detection of what was spurious and unsound. Look, for example, at the masterly way in which he separates the dross from the gold in the work of Byron, of Burns, and in Macpherson's " Ossian "; how he detects the false notes in the Roman poets and in our own poets of the eighteenth century; how admirably in dealing with Dryden he distinguishes between rhetoric and poetry; with what piercing truth he explains the essential differences between poetry of the first order and poetry of the secondary order, the differences which separate Chaucer from Homer, and Dryden from Wordsworth; how sound and illuminating is his analysis of what constitutes excellence in style, his insistence on and illustration of evolution and architecture in a poem on the successful subdual of the details to the total impression; how true and how sound his conception of the aim and functions of true great poetry, " the application of ideas to life." What false conceptions and standards do such a theory sweep away! How noble is this conception of the future of poetry, of what it has the power to effect:

The future of poetry is immense, because in poetry, where it is worthy of its high destinies, our race, as time goes on, will find an ever surer and surer stay. There is not a creed which is not shaken, not an accredited dogma which is not shown to be questionable, not a received tradition which does not threaten to dissolve. Our religion has materialised itself in the fact, in the supposed fact; it has attached its emotion to the fact, and now the fact is failing it. But for poetry the idea is everything: the rest is a world of illusion, of divine illusion. Poetry attaches its emotion to the idea: the idea *is* the fact. The strongest part of our religion to-day is its unconscious poetry.*

Great is our debt to Matthew Arnold. As a man we think of him as he pictured one of his own heroes—Marcus Aurelius: " Wise, just, self-governed, tender, thankful, blameless; yet with all this agitated, stretching out his arms for something beyond — *tendentemque manus ripæ ulterioris amore* "; and this is the image faithfully reflected in his writings. But to those who are still on this side of the bank he left the example of a pure and strenuous life, faithfully and disinterestedly devoted to noble purposes; to lending a helping hand to those who, like himself, needed stays and guidance such as the old creeds and the old traditions could no longer give; to striving to recall a gross and sensual people to worthier standards of taste, of conduct, of aspiration; to vindicating and interpreting the

* Introduction to Ward's "English Poets."

true functions, the divine mission of poetry; to enriching that poetry with many a gem exquisite alike in quality and in conscientious perfection of workmanship; to recalling criticism to a proper sense of its duties and responsibilities, and by furnishing it with models of the ends at which it should aim, of the criteria and methods which it should employ, of the tone, of the accent, of the form in which it may most appropriately and effectually express itself.

BROWNING AND BUTLER

AN ingenious divine of the last century is said to have drawn a parallel between George II. and Enoch; and Fluellen, as we all know, confirmed his comparison of Henry V. and Alexander the Great by pointing triumphantly to the fact that there was a river in Monmouth and a river in Macedon. It may be supposed that, in associating the names of Browning and Butler, I must be aspiring to rival the feat of our George and Enoch friend, and that I propose to amuse my readers with a display of paradoxical ingenuity; but I am not. I detest paradox; and that I may not be put down as a Fluellen, I may explain that the parallel passages which I shall presently adduce are not designed to imply either that their matter is common only to Butler or Browning, or that Browning borrowed from Butler. I am inclined to think that Browning was a reader, and a careful reader, of Butler; but I am quite prepared to admit that what we find in Browning's works common and peculiar to Butler might still have been found in them had he never read a line of the " Analogy " and " Sermons." Why, then, it may be said, institute any comparison at all? My answer to this will explain the scope and purport of this essay. Butler and Browning seem to me to have so much in common that a comparative review of the points of resemblance between them can hardly fail to be at least interesting. Both were men of a very high and a very rare type, of singular purity, simplicity, and honesty ; both were profound and subtle thinkers ; both consummate logicians ; both penetrated in an extraordinary degree with the religious sense ; both brooded painfully and incessantly on the mysteries of life ; both united to the temper of the ruthless logician and philosophical recluse the intensest sympathy with all that calls for sympathy in man's fortune and constitution, being both of them in an eminent degree humane and philanthropic, at once fearless and reverent. Both sought, both yearned, in passion for a solution of life's riddle, for light, for truth, and would not palter. Of both could it be said, in Tennyson's words :

> He fought his doubts and gather'd strength,
>   He would not make his judgment blind,
>   He faced the spectres of the mind
> And laid them : thus he came at length
>
> To find a stronger faith his own ;
>   And Power was with him in the night,
>   Which makes the darkness and the light,
> And dwells not in the light alone.*

Both discerned in the Christian Revelation at least the nucleus, the essence, of what man needed—needed spiritually, needed morally—in the way of support and in the way of inspiration,

* " In Memoriam," xcvi.

and both therefore became its apologists and champions. Neither either acknowledged or felt that, in repelling its assailants, he had advanced a step towards establishing the authenticity and truth of the thing itself; and if Butler, in his scrupulous truthfulness and candour, has raised more doubts than he solved, Browning has left it at least open to debate, if men wish to be nice and curious, whether personally he could be regarded as a Christian or not.

For these reasons, then, have I associated the names of Bishop Butler and Browning. I have myself got so much pleasure and help—I do not mean in a theological sense, but in a general way— from Butler's " Analogy " and " Sermons " that I am glad to dwell on their interest as contributions, not to militant theology, but to the humanities, and to show that writings which are popularly associated only with the groans of candidates for ordination have very real and very precious worth in other spheres of study.

There is one intelligible and consistent theory accordant with reason and accordant with experience on which the scheme, constitution, use, and meaning of man's life on earth may be explained, and that is that it is designed to try and test him, that it is ordained as a period and process of probation.

This idea, I need hardly say, pervades Browning's philosophy of life. It is the kernel of " Rabbi Ben Ezra," is involved in the faith of " Abt Vogler," is the whole burden of " Easter Day," is the deduction of the elaborate logic of

" La Saisiaz," is a leading article in the creed of the Pope in " The Ring and the Book," and finds other expression in poems or in passages of poems too numerous to specify.

Two memorable chapters in Butler's great work, namely, the fourth and fifth, deal most fully and elaborately with this subject, his thesis being :

As the moral government of God which religion teaches us, implies that we are in a state of trial with regard to a future world ; so also His natural government over us implies that we are in a state of trial in the like sense with regard to the present world.

How exactly Browning is on the general question in harmony with Butler will be apparent to any one who will take the trouble to read these two chapters.   Involved in this theory as necessary corollaries are five other leading tenets of Browning's theology, which, for the sake of clearness, may be arranged under separate heads :

(*a*) That a state of probation, being, as it obviously must be, a means of education and discipline, involves the existence and activity of what tends to perplex, impede, and pain us— namely, uncertainty and doubt, evil in various phases, disappointment, affliction and suffering.

(*b*) That this education and discipline extend continuously and progressively through all the stages of life, deepening, broadening, expanding ; always a process, never completed or completing its result, an ungarnered harvest, its effect increasing confidence in the evidence of things unseen.

(*c*) That a necessary corollary of this is the existence of a future life, the protraction of individual consciousness after death ; that death, while it destroys the body, so far from quenching or suspending the activity of the soul, merely alters the conditions very much for the better, under which it exercises its activity.

(*d*) That as progress is the law of the soul's life here on earth, so by analogy we may presume that it will be its law elsewhere, and that, as it passed from point to point, from stage to stage, in development under earthly conditions, such also, presumably, will be its career under unearthly.

(*e*) That individual man—an infinitesimal point in the boundless immensity of God's wholly incomprehensible and unintelligible scheme—has, however, entrusted to him, in the gift of life, a responsibility awful beyond expression ; for, a free agent, what he does or what he fails to do is of concern, not to time only, but to eternity ; not to himself alone, but to the scheme of things ; he can fulfil or he can counteract, so far as he himself is concerned, the law of the soul's life, progressive development.

I proceed to my parallels under the first heading. It will be remembered how often Browning has pointed out the wisdom of Providence in ordaining that doubt and uncertainty should continually disturb and harass us in this life ; that they are not only a part of our probation, but they prevent us from stagnating, brace, nerve, and exercise us ; nay, that without doubt faith could not exist. Bloughram puts this very forcibly. In " La Saisiaz " Browning shows us what would be the result of the substitution of certainty for uncertainty with regard to the question of a future life—either the immediate resignation of this life or absolute indifference to it, or the paralysis of the will. Says St. John :

> Such progress could no more attend his soul
> Were all its struggles after found at first
> And guesses chang'd to knowledge absolute,
> Than motion wait his body, were all else
> Than it the solid earth on every side,
> Where now through space he moves from rest to rest.[*]

And in " Easter Day " its importance as a factor in probationary discipline is elaborately argued.

This is one of Butler's chief points, and he argues it in the sixth chapter of the second part of the " Analogy " :

> The difficulties in which the evidence of religion is involved, which some complain of, are no more a just ground of complaint than the external circumstances of temptation which others are placed in, or than difficulties in the practice of it after a full conviction of its truth. . . . Speculative difficulties are in this respect of the very same nature with these external temptations.

Again :

> What constitutes, what chiefly and peculiarly constitutes, the probation in all senses of some persons may be the difficulties in which the evidence of religion is involved ; and their principal and distinguished trial may be how they will behave under and with respect to these difficulties.

---

[*] " Death in the Desert."

But the two chapters should be compared in detail with Browning.

But life has severer and more drastic discipline for the probationary soul in the form of conflict with evil, of disappointment, apparent failure, suffering and pain. Illustrations of Browning's teaching on this point are needless, because they pervade his works. The note is struck in "Rabbi Ben Ezra":

> Then welcome each rebuff
> That turns earth's smoothness rough,
> Each sting that bids—nor sit—nor stand—but go !
> Be our joys three-parts pain !
> Strive, and hold cheap the strain ;
> Learn, nor account the pang ; dare, never grudge the throe !

and in the prayer of him for whom God in a vision had made the world yield all that the world could yield of comfort and happiness :

> Let that old life seem mine—no more—
> With limitation as before,
> With darkness, hunger, toil, distress :
> Be all the earth a wilderness !
> Only let me go on, go on,
> Still hoping ever and anon
> To reach one eve the Better Land,

and who was content to

> Go through the world, try, prove, reject,
> Prefer, still struggling to effect
> My warfare ; happy that I can
> Be cross'd and thwarted as a man.
> "Christmas Eve" and "Easter Day."

From which flows his oft-repeated paradox, that life may be a failure in being a success, and a success in being a failure. Bishop Butler does not put it so trenchantly, but his views on this point are exactly in harmony with Browning's : as a place of probation only, and as an amply furnished storehouse of the means of probationary discipline, not as a place to be comfortable and happy in, is this world to be regarded. I will not give parallel passages, but will sum up this heading by placing side by side with " Easter Day " a passage from Butler. It is from his sermon upon the Ignorance of Man. The position in Browning's poem is this : Two friends are discussing Christianity. One accepts it through faith, and comments on the difficulty of being a Christian in practice. The other cannot accept it through faith, and expresses his surprise that any one who really believed in its promises should find any difficulty in its practice. In the dialogue which ensues it is shown that the teaching and promises of Christianity are not designed, as the sceptic supposed, to add charm to the world and a zest to mortal life, but rather to wean the soul from earth and to teach it to regard mortal life and the world as means of probationary trial. It is this creed which supports the faith of the Pope, and gives him the key to the spectacle presented by the world :

> I can believe this dread machinery
> Of sin and sorrow, would confound me else,
> Devised,—all pain, at most expenditure
> Of pain by Who devised pain,—to evolve
> By new machinery in counterpart
> The moral qualities of man,—how else ? *

* " Ring and the Book," x. 1374.

Hear Butler :

It is surely reasonable, and what might have been expected, that creatures in some stage of their being, suppose in the infancy of it, should be placed in a state of discipline and improvement where their patience and submission is to be tried by afflictions ; where temptations are to be resisted and difficulties gone through in the discharge of their duty. Now if the greatest pleasures and pains of the present life may be overcome and suspended, as they manifestly may, by hope and fear, and other passions and affections ; then the evidence of religion, and the sense of the consequences of virtue and vice, might have been such as entirely in all cases to prevail over those afflictions, difficulties and temptations ; prevail over them so as to render them absolutely none at all. But the very notion itself now mentioned of a state of discipline and improvement, necessarily excludes such sensible evidence and convictions of religion, and of the consequences of virtue and vice. One condition in this world is a school of exercise for this temper ; and our ignorance, the shallowness of our reason, the temptations, difficulties, afflictions which we are exposed to, all equally contribute to make it so. The general observation may be carried on ; and whoever will attend to the thing will plainly see that less sensible evidence, with less difficulty in practice, is the same as more sensible evidence with greater difficulty in practice. Therefore difficulties in speculation as much come into the notion of a state of discipline as difficulties in practice : and so the same reason or account is to be given of both.

Let us turn now to the second thesis, that this education and discipline extends, continuous and progressive, through all the stages of life—always a process never completed or completing. This is another cardinal article in Browning's teaching. It is the keynote of the " Grammarian's Funeral," is involved in the vision of " Abt Vogler," is the foremost fact to the Pope :

> Life is probation, and the earth no goal,
> But starting-point of man,

is the kernel of "Old Pictures at Florence,"
pervades "Paracelsus," perplexes Cleon, who,
having no assurance or presumption of immortality, is without the key.   It was because the
Rabbi Jochanan Hakkadosh, forgetting that life's
significance lay in its incompleteness, estimated
his actions merely in relation to their supposed
intrinsic value, not remembering that their object
was to keep him working that God might estimate
their worth : it was thus that he would have died
a failure had not childhood given him the true
key.   We need not multiply illustrations.   It is
stated most simply and directly in "Rabbi Ben
Ezra."   The education of youth is the prelude to
that of manhood, that of manhood to that of old
age, old age to that which extends to the moment
of death, when, earthly life having completed its
task, the perfect cup is in the Potter's hand ready
for His use.   Thus there is no interval ; what life
in youth is to life in manhood, and life in manhood
to that of old age, so that of old age is to the life
that shall come *after* death, each life completing
the former.   This is exactly the theory of Butler :

Our existence is not only successive, as it must be of necessity,
but one state of our life and being is appointed by God to be a
preparation for another, and that to be the means of attaining
to another succeeding one, infancy to childhood and childhood
to youth ; youth to mature age.

And thus he concludes :

The former part of life is to be considered as an important opportunity which Nature puts into our hands, and which when lost i

not to be recovered. And our being placed in a state of discipline throughout this life for another world is a providential disposition of things exactly of the same kind as our being placed in a state of discipline during childhood for mature age. Our condition in both respects uniform and of a piece, and comprehended under one and the same general law of Nature.

Thus have both Butler and Browning drawn the same conclusion from the same analogy.

On the third thesis, or series of theses, namely, the existence of a future life; the protraction of individual consciousness after death destroys the body; and the entry of the soul, after it is freed from the shackles of the body, on a fuller life, they are entirely at one. For illustrations from Browning's poems, which would be endless, may be substituted what he wrote to a friend not long before he died:

You know as well as I that death is life, just as our daily, our momentary dying body is none the less alive and ever recruiting new forces of existence; without death there could be no prolongation of that which we call life.

And we all know with what a trumpet note he proclaimed this gospel immortally in verse in one of the last poems he wrote. Under this heading I will merely illustrate from Butler, leaving the reader to recall analogies from Browning:

Of Death :

We cannot argue from the reason of the thing that death is the destruction of living agents, because we know not at all what death is in itself, but only some of its effects. . . . So that there is nothing more certain than that the reason of the thing shows us no connection between death and the destruction of living

o

agents. It destroys the sensible proof which we had before their death of their being possessed of living powers, but does not appear to afford the least reason to believe that they are there, or by that event deprived of them.

Of Life after Death :

Suspension of reason, memory, and the affections which they excite, is no part of the idea of death, nor is implied in our notion of it. . . . So that our posthumous life, whatever there may be in it additional to our present, yet may not be entirely beginning anew, but going on. Death may in some sort and in some respects answer to our birth, which is not a suspension of the faculties which we had before it, or a total change of the state of life in which we existed when in the womb, but a continuation of both, with such and such great alterations. Nay, for aught we know of ourselves, of our present life and of death, death may immediately, in the natural course of things, put us into a higher and more enlarged state of life, as our birth does : a state in which our capacities and sphere of perception and of action may be much greater than at present.

Again :

The constitution of human creatures, and indeed of all creatures which come under our notice, is such that they are capable of naturally becoming qualified for states of life for which they were once wholly unqualified.

And so, like Browning, Butler argues the progressive education and capabilities of man.

Thus—and this leads us to what was comprised under (d)—what is now dark to us in the scheme of things may some day, and under other conditions, become clear ; in other words, we may see completed what we now see only fragmentarily and in tendency. Butler discerns in the scheme of things a tendency towards a perfect system of moral government, and he deduces from this the probability of a completion of that moral government, the existence, in effect, of that of which we here only see the principles and beginning. This is exactly Browning's

On the earth the broken arcs ; in the heaven, a perfect round.

Again, what is " Abt Vogler " but a splendid presentation, in figurate expression, of Butler's remarks in chap. vii. on the probable harmony of God's vast and complex scheme of life, could we view it, not in part, but in totality ?

But nothing links Browning and Butler more closely than their intense consciousness and conviction of the tremendous seriousness of life and the importance of seeking as support some solution of its enigma. It was this which led both of them to realise the momentous importance of the Christian Revelation. They both felt, though in different degrees, how much is involved, or may be involved, in its authenticity or spuriousness, in its rejection or acceptance. Each, satisfied of its divine origin, became, therefore, in simple honesty its strenuous apologist. Butler stood forth as its champion against Toland and Collins, Browning against Strauss and Renan. But the power and, I will add, the charm of the " Analogy " lie quite apart from its relation to religious controversy. They lie not in what it achieved but in what it suggests and reflects. A relic of extinct controversies—with much in it which is outworn and effete—it is yet pregnant with instructive, fertilising, inspiring thought.

And this constitutes its power. Its charm lies in the fidelity with which it reflects the character of its author, his pathetic earnestness, as of one pleading for lives in jeopardy, his scrupulous candour and honesty, his modesty, moderation, and truthfulness, his piety, his philanthropy. As beautiful a soul, as beautiful a character as ever expressed themselves on earth are mirrored in these writings.

Another interesting point of resemblance between Butler and Browning may be found in the distinction which they draw between the sensuous impression of ideas and their subsequent retention and activity independent of bodily organs, and the use to which they have applied this as an argument for posthumous existence. In "A Death in the Desert" Browning describes three souls: the soul that acts; the soul that knows; and the soul that Is. The first two are linked with the body, wax, wane, and perish with it; their use was the use of earth to gather all that can be gathered by sensuous experience in a sensuous sphere: all this passing into essence moulds and makes the "man's self" the soul that Is—and this soul, wholly independent of what death can destroy of what is corporeal, is immortal. Let us turn to the "Analogy," chap. i.:

It is by no means certain that anything which is dissolved by death is in any way necessary to the living being in its state of reflection after ideas are gained. For though from our present constitution and condition of being, our external organs of sense are necessary for conveying in ideas to our reflecting powers . . . yet when these ideas are brought in we are capable of reflecting in the most intense degree, and of enjoying the greatest pleasure and feeling the greatest pain by means of that reflection, without any assistance from our senses, and without any at all, that we know of, from that body which will be dissolved by death. It does not appear, then, that the relation of this gross body to the reflecting being is in any degree necessary to thinking, to our intellectual enjoyments or sufferings; nor, consequently, that the dissolution or alienation of the former by death will be the destruction of those present powers which render us capable of this state of reflection.

I fear our scientific friends will not think this very satisfactory; but with that I am not concerned, nor does it seem to have troubled Browning very much.

Again, both Butler and Browning have, as was very natural in men who were so sincerely anxious to get at truth, commented on the inadequacy of the only medium man has for communicating his thoughts to others—language.

" The imperfections," writes Butler,

attending the only method by which Nature enables and directs us to communicate our thoughts to each other are innumerable. Language is, in its very nature, inadequate, ambiguous, liable to infinite abuse even from negligence, and so liable to it from design that every man can deceive and betray by it.

Says Prince Hohenstiel,

> Do your best,
> Words have to come : and somehow words deflect
> As the best cannon ever rifled will,

and we all know how voluminous a commentary on the remark is supplied us by " The Ring and the Book."

It has been often said that Butler is a pessimist ;

and if that were so, he would, of course, stand in
absolute contrast to Browning. But Butler was
no pessimist. He has, it is true, an air of con-
straint and gloom. He has nothing of the
buoyant confidence of the enthusiast. He seems
himself to feel no satisfaction even when his
arguments are most convincing and his refutation
of error most complete. He seems to have the
embarrassed air of a man delivering a message
without credentials. Of the utter inadequacy of
such means as he had at his command to prove to
others the truth of what he was himself morally
perhaps certain of—the truth of Christianity—
no man was more aware than he. His position
was, indeed, similar to Browning's speaker in
" Fears and Scruples ":

> I can simply wish I might refute you,
>   Wish my friend would,—by a word, a wink,—
> Bid me stop that foolish mouth—you brute you !
>   He keeps absent,—why, I cannot think.

Of all mysteries this seems to him to be the
most perplexing that issues so momentous should,
if the appeal be made to reason, rest on evidence so
slight that it just, and only just, turns the scale
in favour of the probability of Christianity being
true. And yet both Butler and Browning contend that man has light enough given to him to
light his path if he will only use it. This is
beautifully put by Butler :

> The constitution of the world and God's natural government
> over it are all mystery, as much as the Christian Dispensation, yet
> under the first He has given men all things pertaining to life, and
> under the second all things appertaining to godliness.

And this is exactly the position of the Pope in "The Ring and the Book." It is true also that Butler has painted—and few men in darker and more tragic colours—the anarchy and chaos which seem to deform the realm of an omnipotent moral governor. But he was no pessimist. He drew exactly the same conclusion as Browning : he never doubted clouds would break ; never dreamed, though right were worsted, wrong would triumph :

> The moral government of God is exercised by gradually con-ducting things so in the course of His providence that every one at length, and upon the whole, shall receive according to his deserts ; and neither fraud nor violence, but truth and right, shall finally prevail.—Part II. ch. iv.

If this is not optimism, what is ?

BROWNING AND MONTAIGNE

A CERTAIN Peter Bunel, an eminent scholar from Toulouse, had been staying with Montaigne's father, and gave him at parting a book entitled *Theologia Naturalis*, written by one Raymond de Sebonde towards the end of the fifteenth century. It was written in a jargon of Latin and Spanish, and Bunel gave it to Montaigne's father because he thought it might fortify his faith at a time when the novel doctrines of Luther were getting into vogue. But it got mislaid till shortly before the death of the elder Montaigne, when it was found. Then he gave it to his son, and asked him to translate it for him into French, that he might be able to read it.

So young Montaigne went to work and translated it. This led him to dwell seriously on the great problem of the relation of faith to reason, and the whole of this long essay elaborately demonstrates the utter impotence of human reason when it attempts to deal with supernatural truths—in other words, with the truths of Christianity, and the necessity for basing religion on faith and on faith alone. His own position, not in the essay only, but in all his essays, is that of an orthodox son of the Church. Thus, in the essay on Prayers:

Let what I here set down meet with correction or applause, it shall be of equal welcome and utility to me, myself beforehand condemning as absurd and impious, if anything shall be found, through ignorance or inadvertency, couched in this rhapsody, contrary to the holy resolutions and prescripts of the Catholic Apostolic and Roman Church, into which I was born and in which I will die.

This orthodoxy he carried to an extreme, for he would not even allow the words of Scripture to be interpreted otherwise than the authority of the Church interpreted them. He went regularly to chapel, and when he travelled he took every occasion to attend mass. We know how little relation this submission to authority and this punctilious regard for ceremonies generally had in Montaigne's time, and before and since his time, to vital religion; but the essay on "Prayers" forbids us supposing that Montaigne was not sincere. How comes it then that the prince of sceptics, the man who has been claimed by agnostics, and even by atheists, could hold with sincerity this position? It is easily explained. Montaigne based his religion on pure, simple faith and, if such an expression may be allowed, on the dethronement of reason. But when he discussed and speculated he gave the reins to reason. See, he directly or tacitly said, what reason brings us to when it is applied to anything. I am a Christian because I *believe ;* I become anything you like when I speculate, investigate, and inquire. But the particular symbols in which religious belief expresses itself —in Montaigne's case the religion of the Roman

Catholic Church—do not concern it. The point is that religious truths are outside the scope of reason and logic, appealing only to, and concerned solely with, that spiritual faculty or faculties which we call in our imperfect parlance faith. In this essay* he proceeds to show the utter impotence of reason ; that the truths discerned by it can only be relative, that certainty is impossible in anything ; that the mind simply plunges about in shifting quagmires of opinion, or, to change the image, is a mere kaleidoscope.

> The most wretched and frail of all creatures is man, and withal the proudest. He feels and sees himself lodged here in the dirt and filth of the world, nailed and riveted to the worst and deadest part of the universe, in the lowest story of the house, and most remote from the heavenly arch . . . yet in his imagination will be placing himself above the circle of the moon, and bringing heaven under his feet.

And then he goes on to mortify human pride with all that Pope has concentrated so brilliantly in the " Essay on Man " and Swift so savagely and powerfully in " Gulliver's Travels." Taking a comprehensive survey of what man's reason has done, going through the schools of the ancient philosophers, he brings out the melancholy truth that " our wisdom is but folly in the sight of God ; that the vainest of all vanities is man ; that the man who presumes upon his wisdom does not yet know what wisdom is ; and that man, who is nothing, if he thinks himself to be anything, but seduces and deceives himself." He shows how

* " Apology for Raymond de Sebonde."

inconsistent we are with ourselves. He himself, he says, is quite a different man with different views and different opinions at different times. But I need not continue ; whoever would see, summed up as fully and eloquently as it can be, what illustrates these obvious and melancholy truths should turn to this essay. What is his corollary ?

The first law that ever God gave to man was a law of pure obedience ; it was a commandment naked and simple wherein man had nothing to inquire after or to dispute, forasmuch as to obey is the proper office of a rational soul acknowledging a heavenly superior and benefactor. From obedience and sub-mission spring all other virtues, as all sin does from self-opinion. And, on the contrary, the first temptation that by the devil was offered to human nature, its first poison, insinuated itself into us by the promises that were made to us of knowledge and wisdom : " Ye shall be as gods knowing good and evil." . . . The plague of man is the opinion of wisdom ; and for this reason it is that ignorance is so recommended to us by our religion, as proper to faith and obedience.

Again :

Our strength is so far from being able to comprehend the divine height that of the works of our Creator those best bear His mark and are best His which we the least understand. To meet with an incredible thing is an occasion with Christians to believe. It is all the more reason that it is against human reason ; if it were according to reason, it would no longer be a miracle ; if it had an example, it would be no longer a singular thing. . . . 'Tis not by meditation or by virtue of our own understanding that we have acquired our religion . . . 'tis rather by the media-tion of our ignorance than of our knowledge that we know any-thing of the divine Wisdom.

Thus Montaigne shows that not only is reason impotent to guide us to divine truth, but even to throw any steady light on what we call truth in much less important matters.

On *faith* then pure and simple does he base his religion, and there being no medium between believing nothing and believing *all*, he has no difficulty in accepting a religion which, supported as it is by *miracles* and based as it is on the *miraculous*, is an insult to mere reason ; and therefore he is an orthodox Roman Catholic, rejecting Protestantism, which he describes as a compromise between reason and faith.

One great difference between Montaigne and Browning is, of course, this : that while both demonstrate the impossibility of reason probing religious mystery, Montaigne's *faith* leads him to a definite conclusion and creed. Browning has not defined the creed at which he arrives—if he does arrive at a creed at all. Their attitude towards the metaphysics of Christianity is the same : they are beyond and above reason ; they can be reached and apprehended only by faith.

In " La Saisiaz " Browning asks the question, " Was ending ending once and always ? " Which he answers himself by :

Fact 1. Survival in memory. As long as I live, you will ; when I die, then your memory and mine go, and all that then remains will be the continuous life of the race.

Fact 2. Incompleteness of the individual life. But does it follow from this that that life will be completed elsewhere ? Fancy may cherish this belief ; fact is silent. Can I honestly say with Dante, " I believe and I declare—certain am I from this life I pass into a better " ? No, I cannot.

I think therefore *I am I :* there is an object of my thought that is something else. We will call the one the *soul*, we will call the other *God*. These to me are facts. Can I prove them ? *No ;* they are proved to me because they are beyond truth. Here, we see, reason breaks down on the very threshold ; argument even at this early stage would be impossible without a postulate by a faculty which is not reason.

The soul and God are then compared to a rush on a stream—the rush is a fact, the stream is a fact ; but the rush knows not whence the stream flowed from nor where it itself is going, all it knows is that it is now floating down the stream. *I am.* Does it follow that I shall continue to be ? The only certainty is the I on the stream, the middle point ; cause before—blank ; effect behind—blank.

The only truth I can get at is relative, mere surmise, my own experience—that is what seems truth to me. Then the poet goes on to show how to *him*, merely to him with his peculiar temper and experiences, the only intelligible theory of the meaning of life is that it is intended as a place of probation, but this mainly because of the difficulties involved in any theory proceeding on any other assumption than that it is designed with this end.

But, O world spread out beneath me ! only for myself I speak,
Nowise dare to play the spokesman for my brothers strong and
  weak.
       *   *   *   *   *
I shall " vindicate no way of God's to man," nor stand apart,
" Laugh, be candid ! " while I watch it traversing the human
  heart.

Then in a remarkable passage he gives his reasons
for believing this to be the case, selecting for
special argument the fact of the uncertainty of a
future state being permitted to trouble us in
life : Fancy argues on one side, Reason on the
other. Fancy assumes that the immortality of
the soul is certain, and we have got three facts
then : *God is, the soul is* and *shall endure after
death.* Then Reason replies : " *Die at once,* for
a future life would be a very happy exchange for
this life on earth." Then replies Fancy : " I
grant that the certainty of a future life must be
saddled with the having to *endure* and live out
this life." Then replies Reason : " The wise
man will live, but be *indifferent* and lethargic."
Then Fancy has to make another concession.
Man must be impressed with the incalculable
importance of this life ; he must understand
that he wins an eternal heaven or an eternal
hell by his acts in this life. Then replies
Reason : " The freedom of the will would be
paralysed ; he would act virtuously simply to
get an eternal reward, and avoid sin simply
to escape eternal punishment." So we come
back to where we started in this question,
namely, that life seems to be designed as a place

of probation. And with regard to the other questions:

So, I hope—no more than hope, but hope—no less than hope,
  because
 can fathom, by no plumb-line sunk in life's apparent laws,
How I may in any instance fix where change should meetly fall
Nor involve, by one revisal, abrogation of them all:
Which again involves as utter change in life thus law-released,
Whence the good of goodness vanished when the ill of evil ceased.
Whereas, life and laws apparent reinstated,—all we know,
All we know not—o'er our heaven again cloud closes, until, lo—
Hope the arrowy, just as constant, comes to pierce its gloom
  compelled
By a power and by a purpose which, if no one else beheld,
I behold in life, so—hope!
                    Sad summing-up of all to say!

Sad, but what else is possible? How can men's individual fancies and reason guide, I do not say to truth, but to any sort of consistent conclusion? Then, taking the great and famous men associated with the scene near by—Rousseau, Diodati, Byron, Gibbon, Voltaire—he shows the folly of supposing that fame, which seems to be the guarantee for authority, affords any sort of presumption of the possession of extraordinary insight into these questions. What did Voltaire arrive at, he with all his wit, all his genius, all his learning, all his brilliant manifold gifts, all his gigantic Europe-shadowing fame?—just what I, just what so many others have arrived at:

He at least believed in soul, was very sure of God.

Both these facts, as the poet has shown before, are independent of reason: certainly not arrived at through it nor confirmed by it ; they are above and beyond logic.

Very strikingly, then, but quite in a different way, does " La Saisiaz " point to the same conclusion as the "Apology for Raymond de Sebonde." Both works may be easily misunderstood and be pressed into the service of scepticism and agnosticism, and certainly seem in no way designed to serve the religion of which Montaigne was a professed votary and which Browning recognised as a God-sent revelation. But we must not misunderstand them. The foundations of the Christian religion—indeed, the foundations of any true religion—rest on faith, which is a very complex term, and indeed little more than a symbol for spiritual faculties and energies which are too sublime and impalpable for definition. Where reason enters into the sphere of religion it pertains only to its ethical sides ; in other words, to those elements which it has in common with moral philosophy, or, where it touches other sides, can only be regarded as a collateral support. And this is why those who have attempted to bring reason to the defence of the metaphysical truths of Christianity have so commonly failed. Even Bishop Butler breaks down utterly when he attempts to defend the miracles and the supernatural supports of Christianity from the reason of the thing. And yet, as the Bible says (and as Bishop Butler is fond of quoting), " The spirit of man is the candle of the Lord " ;* it may be the ally of faith, but it cannot take its

* Proverbs xx. 27.

place ; it may point, and even guide, us to the higher truths, but it cannot interpret them. In the noblest verses which Dryden ever wrote he described the relation of reason to faith :

> Dim as the borrow'd beams of moon and stars
> To lonely, weary wandering travellers
> Is Reason to the soul : and as on high
> Those rolling orbs discover but the sky,
> Not light us here, so Reason's glimmering ray
> Was lent not to assure our doubtful way,
> But guide us upward to a better day.
> And as those nightly tapers disappear,
> When day's bright lord ascends on hemisphere ;
> So pale grows Reason at Religion's sight ;
> So dies, and so dissolves in supernatural light.*

Surely it is a useful service to reduce reason to its proper place, and this Montaigne and Browning have done.

It may seem strange to bring in " Caliban upon Setebos " in this connection. This wonderfully comprehensive analogue is, of course, primarily intended to satirise those grossly anthropomorphic conceptions of the Deity which we find in pagan and savage mythologies, and also in those theologies in which he was represented not as a God of benevolence and mercy, but as a God of terror ; not as a God to be loved, but as a God to be propitiated. Perhaps it went further, and was intended also to show how vain it is for the finite to suppose that it can comprehend the infinite ; how vain for man to form any more

* " Religio Laici."

P

definite conception of the Deity than is indicated
in the famous passage in "Faust." But the poor
savage is a marvellously comprehensive symbol.
He also reasons and argues, and on his reasons
and arguments bases an elaborate natural theology.
Drawing only on his own observation, his own
experiences, his own instincts and feelings, he
deduces a theology sufficiently absurd and monstrous ; but is he further from the truth than
more refined and cultivated inquirers who have
proceeded on the same method ? Some of his
deductions are identical with those of the Greeks,
namely, the doctrine of the $\phi\theta\acute{o}\nu o s$, of the
jealousy of the gods ; others with those who
have supposed that fasting, votive offerings and
sacrifices can appease the Deity ; in other words,
with those who have conceived of God as though
He were some human tyrant. Indeed, the whole
poem, in evolving the arguments of this ludicrous
savage, is but a grotesque parody of arguments
and deductions—not, it is true, so ridiculous—
which have been expressed in all seriousness by
philosophers and speculators. Caliban's theology
is what it is because, though he has reason—and
indeed he is by no means a bad logician—he has
none of the faculties, even in embryo, which
guide man to religious truth.

There are important points of difference
between Montaigne and Browning. Browning
is intensely serious, and emotion and sentiment
enter very largely into his treatment of those
questions. Montaigne's interest in them seems
to be mainly intellectual, and his tone is often

such that it is sometimes difficult to see whether he is in earnest ; and thus it is quite easy to understand how it is that so many of his own Church have disclaimed him ; how it is that so many schools of heterodox opinion have, on the other hand, annexed him. To Montaigne Christianity was represented only by the Church of Rome ; in no other form did he recognise it. To Browning Christianity was where the spirit of Christ was. With Montaigne there could be no compromise and no distinctions : the whole complicated fabric, the New Testament, orthodox tradition, the decrees of councils, papal authority, and all that found embodiment in the dogma and ritual of his Church stood or fell together. To Browning, as need hardly be said, such a conception was as absurd as it was repulsive ; and if he had any particular sympathy with any particular form of Christianity, it was with the Dissenters. Montaigne delighted in speculation for the mere pleasure of speculation. With Browning speculation originated in profound seriousness, and was directed to the most serious ends. Browning's conception of religion was a purely spiritual one ; in Montaigne it is impossible not to feel that political considerations entered largely into his desire to defend and uphold orthodoxy. " A man would have much ado," he writes, " to make me believe that the sight of our crucifixes, that the picture of our Saviour's piteous passion, that the ornaments and ceremonious motions of our churches, that the voices accommodated to the devotion of our thoughts, and that emotions of the senses do not warm the souls of the people with a religious passion of very advantageous effect."

No doubt these differences are to be, in a large measure, attributed to the different ages in which they lived. But what makes perhaps the greatest of all the differences between them—and it is most significant—is this. No one ever rose from the perusal of Montaigne with any new supports to faith, though he exalted it so highly ; with any increased sense of what humanity owes to the creed for which he professed so much reverence ; rather perhaps with faith shaken and with the feeling that Christianity has been attenuated into a sort of political system and social bulwark. But to how many of us has Browning sent new life-blood pulsing into the old truths ; for how many of us has he rekindled lights that were becoming dim and taught us to understand and feel what Christianity *really means !*

BROWNING AND LESSING

WAS Browning a Christian? Mrs. Sutherland Orr tells us positively that he was not, that he was an agnostic. And Mrs. Orr knew him personally, very intimately, and is also profoundly acquainted with his works. So of two things we may be sure: either that what is meant by the name Christian is so vague and indeterminate that it cannot connote what is ordinarily connoted by it, or that most of the fundamental principles and ideas that pervade his writings when they touch on religious ideas, as well as a large portion of those writings themselves, such as "Saul," "Cleon," "An Epistle of Karshish," "Christmas Eve," "Easter Day," and "A Death in the Desert," are to be regarded as mere aspects of speculative truth and dramatically psychological studies. As for his being an agnostic, the term means anything and indicates nothing at all. Was Lessing a Christian? The superficial answer would be: "Certainly not; for did not he describe 'orthodox Christianity' as 'the most frightful structure of nonsense,' and did he not, when almost on his deathbed, say, 'Call the notary. I will declare before him that I die in none of the prevailing religions'? And was he not at open and furious war with every Christian sect and party in Germany?"

And yet I venture to think that Lessing was a Christian in very essential senses of the term. He certainly believed in the divine origin of Christianity; he believed it to be a revelation of unique importance. He believed that it embodied immortal truths, that it raised the human race on to a higher plane of spiritual and moral activity, from which it would not descend, but along which it would proceed stage by stage ever upward till it reached perfection.

And now how did Lessing fight the battle of Christianity against its assailants, and teach Browning to fight them too ?

In Hamburg, when Lessing was living there, died Hermann Samuel Reimarus, a professor of Oriental languages and an eminent scholar. He was a Deist, and had long been occupied with a series of works of a most heterodox character ; but he was a timid man, and had not ventured to publish any of them. Lessing had become acquainted with the daughter of Reimarus, and she placed the MSS. in his hands. The principal treatise of Reimarus was an " Apology for Reasonable Believers in God," which was written in a spirit of intense hostility to Christianity. Lessing did not agree with many of the opinions expressed in it, but he believed it would be a good thing to give the work to the world, first, because it would further the cause of religious toleration ; and, secondly, because it would put the believers in Christianity on their mettle. But it was impossible to get the work published because of the severe censorship exercised over the press at

Berlin. However, at Brunswick he got permission
to publish some fragments from other papers of
Reimarus. He began in 1774 with the " Toleration of Deists." This was succeeded by other
fragments, to which he gave the general title of
" Something More from the Papers of the
Anonymous Writer concerning Revelation."
There were five papers in all. They contained
attacks on the credibility of the Old Testament
and of the New as daring as Voltaire's, or as any
which have been made since. One of them comments on the contradictions of the Evangelists in
their account of the Resurrection, contending that
the Resurrection was a fable, that the disciples
carried Christ's body away and deliberately
deceived the world by a fictitious narrative.

Thus Reimarus anticipated Strauss and modern
historians. To put it comprehensively, he
attempted to demolish the historical foundations of
Christianity, and in thus shaking or demolishing its
foundations he imagined that he was demolishing
Christianity itself; that it was attached to historical
fact, and that with the failure of the fact what was
attached to it would collapse. Of the enormous
sensation which the publication of these papers
made and of the controversies in which they
involved Lessing I need say nothing. What concerns us are the commentaries which Lessing
published with these Reimarus fragments. With
many of the opinions of Reimarus he was by no
means in accordance, and his attitude is that of
an apologist for Christianity against the attacks
of Reimarus—just the position of Browning. He

protests against the confusion between faith and
reason, which are constantly assumed to be one,
whereas they are not one but entirely different.
He says that reason once for all accepts revelation, and that, having done so, it has no right to
require that the mysteries of religion shall be
made intelligible, as Reimarus had required.
Reimarus had assumed that because the Old
Testament does not teach the immortality of the
soul it could not be regarded as a revelation.
Lessing asks why a revelation should be supposed
to communicate absolute final truth. God taught
man by degrees, His teachings being adapted to
that stage in intelligence and culture reached by
those to whom they were communicated. Here
he develops the theory advanced in his " Education of the Human Race "—of a progressive
revelation. Then with regard to the attacks on
the credibility of the witnesses on the subject
of the Resurrection, he argues that the contradictions are not those of the actual witnesses, but
those who report what the actual witnesses had
seen ; and that if they did contradict themselves, as very likely the actual witnesses would
have done, that would prove nothing, for no
witnesses give precisely the same account of what
they have seen. Then Lessing flashes into this
(note it carefully for our purpose) :

The broad fact is that the cause which depended upon the
credible evidences of these witnesses is won. Christianity has
triumphed over the Heathen and Jewish Religions. *It is here.*

But the grand key passage is this :

Suppose all the objections urged in the Fragments were proved to be well founded, suppose it were necessary to give up the Bible altogether, what then ? Would it be necessary also to give up Christianity ? By no means. The theologian might be perplexed : the Christian would remain unaffected. What has the Christian to do with the hypotheses, the explanations, the proofs of the theologian ? To him it is once for all there, the Christianity which he feels to be so true and in which he feels himself so happy. If the paralytic experiences the beneficial shock of the electric spark, what does it matter to him whether Nollet or Franklin or neither of them is right ? In short, the letter is not the spirit and the Bible is not religion. Consequently, accusations against the letter and the Bible are not also accusations against the spirit and against religion.

In his " Education of the Human Race," which also grew out of this controversy, his main thesis is that what education is to the individual, revelation is to the race. Education is revelation coming to the individual man, and revelation is education which has come and is yet coming to the human race. The first revelation God gave was a conception given to an individual of the one God. Next He selected an individual people— the Hebrew people—and revealed Himself to them as the God of their nation : the one God, not teaching them the immortality of the soul, for they were not ripe for it, but the doctrine of rewards and punishment on earth. So familiarising them with Himself under these conditions, He fitted them for the further revelation which came with Christ, who was the first certain practical teacher of the immortality of the soul, making that the central point in His teaching. So mankind went on in progressive education, from primer to primer, in each of which they were successively drilled, till they were fitted for the next. On what lines will the further development for the next revelation proceed ? He sees one of the germs of it in the doctrine of the Trinity. How, he says, if this doctrine should at last, after endless errors, bring men on the road to recognise that God cannot possibly be one in the sense in which finite things are one, that even His unity must be a transcendental unity which does not exclude a sort of plurality ? But in some form, developing out of the old, this further revelation will assuredly come—the time of a new eternal gospel which is promised us in the primer of the New Testament itself.

But is it not here with us now, this further revelation which Lessing thus anticipated, and has it not come in the form in which he anticipated it would come—namely, in the increasing subordination of what may be called the accidents of Christianity to its essence; in the increasing indifference to dogma, to the niceties of ritual, to all that we mean by "the letter"; in the proportionately increasing sense of the power and beauty of the spirit, of the substance; in the gradually predominating conviction that Christianity means neither this body of dogmas nor that, neither this institution and system nor that; means not the scaffoldings of the initiatory stages of the early fabric, nor the accretions, doctrinal, political, and otherwise, which have gathered on it since; but the acceptance of God in Christ, this and all that this involves practically.

in conduct, inspiringly in aspiration and endeavour, spiritually in faith ?

Thus is Christianity, the shackles fettering it
to this form or that form gradually falling off,
expanding illimitably, mingling itself, though
without losing its identity, with universal truth.

This is the Christianity of Lessing and Browning. If we turn to what we will, turn now to
" A Death in the Desert," we shall see how much
there is in common between them as apologists
of Christianity, and how much Browning is
apparently indebted to Lessing. If he was not,
the parallels are at least interesting. Their
position and purpose are similar. Lessing urged
his arguments in defence of Christianity against
the attacks of Reimarus; Browning against the
attacks of Strauss and his school. Reimarus and
Strauss supposed that in demolishing the historical
foundations of Christianity they were destroying
the thing itself. Lessing and Browning contended
that the truth of Christianity is independent of
its historical proof. What concerns us now is not
how we got Christianity and how it grew up, but
that *we have it*. Take an illustration of Browning's.
Prometheus, says the fable, stole fire from heaven.
Well, if he did, he did. There were various traditions about his having stolen the fire, and serious
discrepancies in them. What does it matter ?
We have got fire. Are we going to reject fire
because we are not satisfied about its origin and
find inconsistencies in the traditions about its
origin ?   Are we going to reject Christianity
because we are not satisfied with evidence which

we are absolutely incompetent to investigate and estimate, though we have the thing itself, a living, energising fact—a step in the ladder of progress on which we must mount if we are to ascend ?

John saw Christ, heard, touched Him.   *Soul that does.*

What he saw and heard was registered on and by the next faculties, which also used that knowledge, reflected on it, willed on it.   *Soul that knows.*

All these moulded and made what constitutes the spiritual personality, the immortal " I " which survives death.   *Soul that is.*

The first two fade and perish with the body ; the last is the imperishable " I."

To put it more clearly :

Christ was seen and heard by His disciples : there was once, then, testimony—the testimony of the soul that does. They reflected on what they had seen and heard—then was the testimony of the soul that knows. That has passed away with them and with their mortal life. But there is also what Christianity effected and accomplished, what it moulded and made of them—the testimony of the soul that is.

St. John thinks how will it be with a belief in Christ in the future, when the testimony of the soul that does and the soul that knows is no longer possible. He has had an indication even in his own lifetime.

" When," he said, " I heard and saw Christ—
gave men the testimony of the soul that does—
men believed. When I gave them the testimony
of the soul that knows they also believed. But
when I taught the truth in itself, thinking that
it could go on and make way on its own strength,
refuting doubts by its own intrinsic virtue and
power, I found I made no impression. So I found
that men attached more importance to the fact
that I saw Christ and was inspired at Patmos
than to the testimony of the truth itself. In the
far future men will perhaps question whether
ever I existed, whether I ever saw what I did
see, and will reject the truth because it is not
proved by the testimony of personal assurance,
by the testimony of the soul which is even now
failing me." To him close on physical dissolution,
with the material veil which intervenes between
the spirit and spiritual truth thinning and falling
off, *all* is clear—the miracle of Christ's life and
death, the need and the transcendency of sin
and death, the ubiquity of God's love in the
world; in a word, the truth and the power of
Christ's message—all this to *him* is needing not
the testimony of the soul that acts or the soul
that knows, for now all is clear to the vision of
the soul that is. " But to you," addressing his
disciples, " to you, before whose soul is the veil of
the flesh, the veil of youth and strength, how
shall I make it clear ? I must furnish you, as it
were, with an optic-glass which shall enable you
to see, succinct, distinct, small, and clear, in proper
perspective, not the grand universal, immense

truth in all its universality and immensity, but that truth contracted, as it were, to plain historic fact: *that* having been made plain and realised, then you will have the vision of what I have."

Life is given us that we may learn the truth; but the soul does not learn as the flesh does: the flesh grasps it at once. Man needs no second proof of the worth of fire; he troubles himself nothing about Prometheus and tradition, but accepts it at once. But spiritual truths are not accepted like that. We may know the worth of Christ as we know the value of fire, but we cannot in the same way grasp this truth in our lives.

Then St. John goes on to anticipate the objections which will be raised in the far future against his gospel. They will say, "Your tales are not proved—miracles that prove doctrine go for naught. You say that Christ embodied love and power; but, accepting the incarnation of love and power, does it follow that the divine Christ existed? Man, having that affection in his heart, may have read it into a fable, just as man did in his mental infancy read his own emotions and conceptions into Nature." These objections St. John then answers on the lines of Lessing's treatise: "I say that man was made to grow, not to stop." What helped him when he needed help is withdrawn when its end is served, and nothing shall prove twice what once was proved. The truth needed the help of miracles, as a garden plot with young seeds in it is protected with twigs. When the herbs wave, it is no longer for old twigs you look. The miracles were wrought as a matter of fact ; but what concerns mankind is not the truth of the miracles, but the truth originally confirmed and aided by the miracles— the acknowledgment of God in Christ.

> Wouldst thou unprove this to re-prove the prov'd ?
> In life's mere minute, with power to use that proof,
> Leave knowledge and revert to how it sprung ?
> Thou hast it ; use it and forthwith or die.*

Exactly Lessing's argument, you will remember.

> For I say, this is death and the sole death,
> When a man's loss comes to him from his gain,
> Darkness from light, from knowledge ignorance,
> And lack of love from love made manifest.†

Suppose when God gave the first revelation man needed—namely, that *there was a Might* behind the might of Nature, God Himself—man had said, " Since all is might, what use of will ? " and had become merely apathetic. When God gave him the second revelation—namely, that there was love behind the might—is he going to turn round and say, when he sees love every-where :

> Since such love is everywhere,
> And since ourselves can love and would be loved,
> We ourselves make the love, and Christ was not—

rejecting Christ " through very need of Him " ? If he does so,

> The lamp o'erswims with oil, the stomach flags,
> Loaded with nurture, and that man's soul dies.

---

* " Death in the Desert."   † Ibid.

But why, it may be asked, did God perplex the revelation of truth by presenting it in such an unsatisfactory form ? The answer is, because man can only be educated gradually ; he must gain truth circuitously, pass from old to new, from vain to real, from mistake to fact ; his distinctive mark is the capacity for progress :

> Lower than God who knows all and can all,
> Higher than beasts which know and can so far
> As each beast's limit, perfect to an end.

And this progress would be impossible under other conditions than the conditions under which he is placed with respect to action and with respect to education :

> God's gift was that man should conceive of truth
> And yearn to gain it, catching at mistake,
> As midway help till he reach fact indeed.

If we reject such truth as we are under these conditions able to acquire, the penalty on us will be that we shall never attain the ultimate truth.

So St. John anticipates and answers those who would reject Christianity because those were the conditions under which it was presented to us.

Browning is here, as in many other parts of his writings, developing the grand passage in Lessing's " Duplik " :

Not the truth of which a man is or believes himself to be possessed but the sincere effort he has made to come behind the truth makes the worth of the man. For not through the possession but through the investigation of truth does he develop those energies in which alone consists his ever-growing perfection. Possession makes the mind stagnant, indolent, proud. If God held enclosed in His right hand all Truth, and in His left simply the ever-moving impulse towards Truth, although with the condition that I should always be erring, and said to me : " Choose ! " I should humbly bow before His left hand and say, " Father, give from this. Pure Truth is for Thee alone."

How far all this is satisfactory we must each decide for ourselves. To many, and probably to very many, Browning's thesis and arguments will seem, in the main at least, a tissue of unwarrantable hypotheses and equally unwarrantable conclusions, and to raise exceedingly ingenious exercise in logical dialectic but little more. To many it will probably appear that all which is worth serious consideration in his argument is what he has in common with Lessing, and this is surely important. It was not a sophistical answer to the school of Reimarus and Strauss to say that the truth of Christianity depends on testimony which historical and philological criticism cannot shake, and that the Christian can afford to concede the justice of much which his opponents have urged against the authenticity of the Bible without any apprehension as to the soundness of the credentials of his creed. Again, Lessing's theory of a progressive revelation, also adopted by Browning, is such as must recommend itself to most thoughtful people. It finds so much corroboration in obvious facts: it suggests so much: it explains so much.

TENNYSON*

THE ancients who are our masters in everything which relates to Art and Belles Lettres have recognised two distinct functions in poetry—to please and to instruct.

It pleases as a medium of sensuous impression—through rhythmic harmony, through appeals to emotion, to imagination, to fancy: it pleases because it gives form, voice and language to what as human beings, we all feel or think or see without being able adequately to express or define—because it gives, as it were, eyes to the purblind and articulate expression to the half dumb: because it recalls our best and highest moods and moments, or brings back to us sweet and tender memories or ecstasies and passions which once thrilled us in experience: because it brings before us in all their charm and power what is implied in the Beautiful, and what is implied in the Ideal, because it raises us above our ordinary level, and appeals to the divinity within us. Says Bacon:

Poesy is a part of learning . . . which, being not tied to the law of matter may, at pleasure join that which Nature hath severed and sever that which Nature hath joined. It is . . . nothing

---

* Those quotations which are still copyright are given by permission of Messrs. Macmillan and Co.

else but Feigned History. . . . The use of this Feigned History
hath been to give some shadow of satisfaction to the mind of
man in those points wherein the nature of things doth deny it;
the world being in proportion inferior to the soul; by reason
whereof there is agreeable to the spirit of man a more ample
greatness, a more exact goodness . . . than can be found in
the nature of things. . . . It doth raise and erect the mind by
submitting the shows of things to the desires of the mind, whereas
reason doth buckle and bow the mind unto the nature of things.*

And these are the reasons why poetry gives
pleasure. This is the secret of the power
exercised over us by such notes as:

> Break, break, break
> On thy cold gray stones, O Sea!
>
> *   *   *
>
> But the tender grace of a day that is dead
> Will never come back to me.

or as:

Thou hast made him a little lower than the angels and hast
crowned him with glory and honour.

But poetry has other functions than these,
functions which it exercises through these media,
but which are other than they. It teaches us to
solve the three great problems of existence.
What do we know—what must we do—for what
may we hope?

It was believed in ancient times that God, one
form under many names, spoke through the lips
of inspired poets, that they appeared generation
after generation a perpetual witness to Him,
vindicating His will, interpreting His dispensation, that in the light of divine wisdom they read
human nature and human life, and that it was

* "Advancement of Learning," Bk. II.

their office not only to teach man his duties to God, to the State and to himself, but to strengthen and temper him for their fulfilment. " Children," says Aristophanes, " have the schoolmaster to teach them, but when men are grown up the poets are their teachers." The poet, says Ben Jonson, is

able to inform young men to all good disciplines, inflame grown men to all great virtues, keep old men in their best and supreme state, or as they decline to childhood recover them to their first strength ; that comes forth the interpreter and arbiter of nature, a teacher of things divine no less than human, a master in manners ; and can alone, or with a few, effect the business of mankind.*

And in thus expressing himself, Ben Jonson is but expressing the common opinion of antiquity on the nature of the poet's office, on the high duties to which the poet is called, is but expressing what Cicero, what Ovid, what Horace, what Juvenal, what other classical authors have in celebrated passages expressed almost in the same terms. " My father," says Nicêratus, in Xenophon, " anxious that I should become a good man, made me learn all the poems of Homer by heart, for if any of us, he said, wishes to become a prudent ruler of his house or an orator or a general or a public servant, let him know Homer well." " The poets," says another Greek author, " are the common tutors and teachers of all Greece." " Poetry," said Valerius Maximus, " is of more benefit to the young than all the lectures of the Greek Philosophical Schools." And he even attributes to its influence the virtues of Camillus

* Dedication prefixed to " Volpone, or the Fox."

and Fabricius. It was this view of poetry that Lord Chatham took when he wrote to his nephew at Cambridge: " I hope you taste now and love Homer and Virgil. You cannot read them too much, they are not only poets but they contain the finest lessons we can learn, lessons of honour, courage, disinterestedness, love of truth, command of temper, gentleness of behaviour, humanity, and in one word, virtue in its true signification." This is the view which we ought to take of the chief end and use of poetry. Let us not accustom ourselves to think of it as illusion, still less to understand by it what Pater and his school tell us that we ought to understand by it, viz. " all literary production which attains the power of giving pleasure by its form as distinct from its matter," but to have quite other notions of what is to be understood by poetry.

Tennyson makes noble use of poetry when he puts into the mouth of Pallas Athene such lines as these :

> Self-reverence, self-knowledge, self-control,
> These three alone lead life to sovereign power,
> Yet not for power (power of herself
> Would come uncalled for) but to live by law,
> Acting the law we live by without fear ;
> And because right is right, to follow right
> Were wisdom in the scorn of consequences.*

Tennyson's political creed and teaching are those of a liberal conservative in the true, in the best sense of the term. In the happy equilibrium of the three powers: the Crown, the aristocracy,

* " Œnone."

and the people—monarchy, oligarchy, democracy, and of the elements involved in these institutions he finds what will be the secret of happiness for the

> land that freemen till,
> That sober-suited Freedom chose,
> The land where girt with friend or foes
> A man may speak the thing he will;
> A land of settled government,
> A land of just and old renown,
> Where Freedom slowly broadens down
> From precedent to precedent.*

> Love thou thy land with love far-brought
> From out the storied Past, and used
> Within the Present, but transposed
> Thro' future time by power of thought.

But he is no bigot, he is always just and reasonable and denounces alike the vices and defects of both orders, the unworthy exaltation of mere caste and of what may simply be the result of nothing but accidents of fortune in "Lady Clara Vere de Vere," and in "Aylmer's Field." We all know the lines:

> Howe'er it be, it seems to me,
> 'Tis only noble to be good.
> Kind hearts are more than coronets,
> And simple faith than Norman blood.

While on the other hand he ridicules the theory that there is nothing in descent.

Even the homely farmer can teach us there is something in descent.

---

* "You ask me why, tho' ill at ease."

and almost savagely unmasks democratic cant about men being " equal."

> Envy wears the mask of Love, and laughing sober fact to scorn,
> Cries to Weakest as to Strongest, " Ye are equals, equal-born."
> Equal-born ? O yes, if yonder hill be level with the flat.
> Charm us, Orator, till the Lion look no larger than the Cat.*

And so in his late years he broke with the advanced radical party, not because he was less liberal, but because they have become extravagant. It was " Forward, forward," fifty years ago, but of late he saw

> Chaos, Cosmos ! Cosmos, Chaos ! once again the sickening game ;
> Freedom, free to slay herself, and dying while they shout her
> name.†

He was no more inconsistent than Burke. Refined good sense, sobriety and moderation distinguish his political teaching as they distinguish all his teaching. Always on the side of rational progress, there was not a really liberal movement in which he was not in the van. Always against unreason and folly, he denounces the insanity of entrusting power to those who are not fitted to exercise it. As patriotic as Shakespeare, never has England had a more loyal, a more devoted son—how he loves her ! how he glories in her great sons and in her great achievements. We all know the noble ballads written as it were in fire, in which her soldiers and her sailors will find their most lasting monument.

---

* " Locksley Hall Sixty Years After."   † Ibid.

English to the core, he was never an aggressive patriot, though he opposed timidity and pusillanimity when the occasion seemed to warrant prompt action. Precious indeed is his political teaching, for it is as sound sentimentally as it is sound in simple reason, and this is nowhere better exemplified than in the two striking and beautiful passages which denote his attitude as regards the relation of women to the scheme of life.*

In the character of the Prince's mother in the

---

* Man for the field and woman for the hearth :
Man for the sword and for the needle she :
Man with the head and woman with the heart :
Man to command and woman to obey ;
All else confusion.

—" Princess," v. 437.

For woman is not undevelopt man,
But diverse : could we make her as the man,
Sweet Love were slain : his dearest bond is this,
Not like to like, but like in difference.
Yet in the long years liker must they grow ;
The man be more of woman, she of man ;
He gain in sweetness and in moral height,
Nor lose the wrestling thews that throw the world ;
She mental breadth, nor fail in childward care,
Nor lose the childlike in the larger mind ;
Till at the last she set herself to man,
Like perfect music unto noble words ;
And so these twain, upon the skirts of Time,
Sit side by side, full summ'd in all their powers,
Dispensing harvest, sowing the To-be,
Self-reverent each and reverencing each
Distinct in individualities,
But like each other ev'n as those who love.

—" Princess," vii. 259

" Princess," and of Edith in " Aylmers Field," he has given us his ideal of what woman should be.

Tennyson's ethics and religion as revealed in his poetry are that our education should be based on reverence and faith.

> Make knowledge circle with the winds ;
>> But let her herald, Reverence, fly
>> Before her to whatever sky
> Bear seed of men and growth of minds.
>> —" Love Thou thy Land."

Again in " The Ancient Sage " :

> And cling to Faith beyond the forms of Faith !
> She reels not in the storm of warring words,
> She brightens at the clash of " Yes " and " No,"
> She sees the Best that glimmers thro' the Worst,
> She feels the Sun is hid but for a night,
> She spies the summer thro' the winter bud,

So

> We have but faith, we cannot know.[*]

And it is in the apparent decadence of faith and reverence that he sees the worst symptom of our times.

For these are the new dark ages, you see, of the popular press,
When the bat comes out of his cave, and the owls are whooping
    at noon,
And Doubt is the lord of the dunghill and crows to the sun and
    the moon,
Till the Sun and the Moon of our science are both of them turned
    into blood,
And Hope will have broken her heart, running after a shadow of
    good.[†]

---

[*] " In Memoriam," line 21.   [†] " Despair."

The poet is no less emphatic on the subject of the necessity for self-renunciation and devotion to duty. How powerfully has he shown us in the "Palace of Art" that man is not and cannot be self-sufficing: that without humility and self-sacrifice all that this world can give will be of no avail. How fearfully has he illustrated in the "Vision of Sin," and in the tragedy of Guinevere and Lancelot, the havoc which may be wrought through the sins of the senses.

Duty must be our watchword:

> The toppling crags of Duty scaled
> Are close upon the shining tablelands
> To which our God Himself is moon and sun.

All through the Ode on Wellington this is the key—his sense of duty, his truthfulness. So again in the "Charge of the Light Brigade":

> Theirs not to make reply,
> Theirs not to reason why,
> Theirs but to do and die:
> Into the Valley of Death
> Rode the six hundred.

And more perhaps than any poet has he won his way to the hearts of his contemporaries for having entered fully into the spiritual life of his time—into its doubts, its fears, its hopes; and not only do these emotions find tender and graceful expression in his poetry, but he has taught us, taught us not dogmatically or intrusively, but gently and suggestively, how those doubts may be best solved, how those fears may be best dispelled, how those hopes may be best kept alive. As long as human nature shall remain the same, and death and calamity and sorrow be busy in the world, it is not likely that what is essential in the teaching and promises of the Founder of Christianity will lose their dominion over men. But though the text remains the same, the commentary will be always changing. What one age interprets literally, another interprets symbolically. Each age surveys and will survey the great creed from its own medium. And sometimes the starry firmament which it has stretched over human life will be well-nigh obliterated by earth's clouds. Never perhaps has the prospect been blacker than now. Matthew Arnold described the position of hundreds of thousands when he wrote :

" At the present moment two things about the Christian religion must surely be clear to anybody with eyes in his head. One is that men cannot do without it ; the other that they cannot do with it as it is." *

How are the grand central doctrines of Christianity to be reconciled with the facts of science, with evolutionism. That is the problem. Let us see how Tennyson grapples with it.

He leaves its dogmatic side alone—the *letter* killeth but the *spirit* giveth life. God is a God of Love. Christ's *essential* teaching is wholly adequate ; Christianity satisfies man's spiritual instincts and needs. Man cannot do without God, for he is not and cannot be self-sufficing. That is the teaching of his poetry, and nowhere is

* Preface to " God and the Bible."

it better expressed than in " In Memoriam."
In " Lucretius " and in " Despair " he has given
pictures of what may be the end of a life without
God.

On the question of evolution Tennyson, true
to the poet's high mission, has vindicated the
dignity of man, and shown that be Nature's
message what it may, it is not from *Her* that
man's gospel comes.   What though

> I found him not in world or sun
>   Or eagle's wing or insect's eye ;
>   Nor thro' the questions men may try,
> The petty cobwebs we have spun : *

No—

> *Love* is and was my King and Lord
>   And will be, tho' as yet I keep
>   Within his court or earth, and sleep
> Encompass'd by his faithful guard,
>
> And hear at times a sentinel
>   Who moves about from place to place,
>   And whispers to the worlds of space,
> In the deep night, that all is well.
>
> And all is well, tho' faith and form
>   Be sunder'd in the night of fear ;
>   Well roars the storm to those that hear
> A deeper voice across the storm.†

But a worshipper of truth and no bigot, he has
steadily confronted and taught us also to confront
steadily whatever science may decipher ; be the
origin of our physical tabernacle what it may, our

* " In Memoriam," cxxiv.   † Ibid. cxxvi, cxxvii.

origin as *men* dates not from that but from the moment when our Maker

Sent the shadow of Himself, the boundless, thro' the human *soul*.*

And evolutionism, in the sense of continuous development of progression onwards, he does accept. A seer he did stand on a Pisgah from which he describes the crowning race—the race

> Of those that, eye to eye, shall look
>   On knowledge ; under whose command
>   Is Earth and Earth's, and in their hand
>   Is Nature like an open book. †

As a young man he wrote :

Yet I doubt not thro' the ages, one increasing purpose runs,
And the thoughts of men are widened with the process of the suns.‡

Never has he lost sight of the realisation of

> That God, which ever lives and loves,
> One God, one law, one element
> And one far-off divine event,
> To which the whole creation moves.§

And only a few months before our seer and poet " crossed the Bar " he proclaimed :

Man as yet is being made, and ere the crowning age of ages,
Shall not æon after æon pass and touch him into shape ?
All about him shadow still, but while the races flower and fade,
Prophet-eyes may catch a glory slowly gaining on the shade,
Till the peoples all are one, and all their voices blend in choric
Hallelujah to the Maker. " It is finished. Man is made." ‖

---

* " Locksley Hall Sixty Years After."
† " In Memoriam," Con. 128.   ‡ " Locksley Hall."
§ " In Memoriam," last stanza.   ‖ " The Making of Man."

One other point, his profound seriousness—
the σπουδαιότης of Pindar, Dante and Milton—
how soon all must be over for us—how dreamlike
is life:

> We pass : the path that each man trod
>   Is dim, or will be dim, with weeds ;
> What fame is left for human deeds
> In endless age ?   It rests with God.*

And how paltry are our feuds and quarrels:

> Ah God ! the petty fools of rhyme
>   That shriek and sweat in pigmy wars
> Before the stony face of Time,
>   And looked at by the silent stars :
>
> And strain to make an inch of room
>   For their sweet selves, and cannot hear
> The sullen Lethe rolling doom
>   On them and theirs and all things here.†

Surely we have a noble teacher here, and when
we have come to approach poetry as we ought to
approach it, and to bring it into the same relation
with life as the ancients brought it ; to seek in it
a stay and a solace, a stimulus and an inspiration
as we may do, we English shall find in this great
man what few of our countrymen can supply.

It may be—but that posterity will decide—
that what appeals to our day, to us as a nation,
preponderates over what is of permanent and
universal interest and importance to all ages and
peoples, and that in the Valhalla of the Future

---

* " In Memoriam," lxxiii.   † " Literary Squabbles."

he will not take his place among the classics of the human race—still of one thing we may be sure, that no name will ever be more loved and honoured in that Island and by that race for which he had so great an affection, and for which he so nobly wrought.

CURIOSITIES OF POPULAR PROVERBS

THE curiosities of proverbs begin with their definition, for curious it is that of the innumerable definitions which have been given of them, not one of them can be regarded as satisfactory, and that the best of all should have been flashed out, on the spur of the moment, at a London breakfast-table. This was Lord John Russell's famous "Wisdom of many and wit of one," or, in its original form, "One man's wit and all men's wisdom." If we compare this with its predecessors its felicity will at once be apparent. Aristotle's and Plutarch's are too poor to be quoted ; that given by Erasmus is neat, but essentially inadequate, "Celebre dictum scitâ quâpiam novitate insigne" ("A popular saying distinguished by any witty novelty"). Nor does Cornelius Agricola much help us with his "Short sentences into which, as in rules, the ancients have compressed life " ; or Camden's "Concise, witty and wise speeches grounded upon long experience, containing for the most part good caveats, and therefore most profitable and delightful " ; or Ray's lumbering 'Short sentence or phrase in common use, containing some trope, figure, homonymy, rhyme, or other novity of expression." As for James

Howell's "A great deal of weight wrapt up in a little," Fuller's "Much matter decocted into few words," and Dr. Johnson's "Short sentence frequently repeated by the people," they merely play with the accidents of definition. Nor does Archbishop Trench much advance matters when he tells us that "Shortness, sense and salt" must enter into their composition. For some proverbs have salt without sense, some sense without salt; and even if we concede the existence of all these qualities, as in the composition of most proverbs we must do, we have still left a proverb undistinguished from an epigram, and Lord John Russell, so far as definition goes, is master of the field.

An Elizabethan dramatist has observed that one poet is another's plagiary, and he a third's, until they all end in Homer. There is a touch of exaggeration in this, of course; but, allowing for a similar touch of exaggeration, it may be said of the proverbs most current in modern Europe that they may be traced to the wit and wisdom of ancient Greece and Rome. A large percentage have been directly derived from the classics; a still larger percentage have been deduced in various degrees of modification from them. Some, perhaps many, have no doubt sprung up independently, being original deductions from experience and observation, but, coinciding with those of antiquity, have become indistinguishable from them. The history of hundreds of them is very similar. In their first form the truth expressed is stated simply; it then assumes figurative

R

expression variously embodied, and perhaps gains vogue by being quoted or applied on some historically memorable occasion. Take for example, "One beats the bush, and another catches the bird." In its earliest form we find it in Hesiod, who says of drones, "Into their own belly they scrape together the labour of another" (ἀλλότριον κάματον σφετέρην ἐς γαστέρ' ἀμῶνται). Then we find it as "Some have laboured, others profited" (ἄλλοι κάμον, ἄλλοι ὤναντο). Then it appears in the New Testament, "One soweth, another reapeth," having already figured in the Talmud as "One says grace, and another eats." Next, with the image altered, we have it in Old French, "Il bat le buisson sans prendre l'oisillon," and in Spanish, "Uno levanta la caza y otro la mata"; in Italian another turn is given to it, "I piccioli cani trovano, mà i grandi hanno la lepre" ("The little dogs find, but the big ones have the hare"). It was then applied on a memorable occasion by Henry V., who, on it being proposed to give up Orleans to the Duke of Burgundy, then in the English camp, said indignantly, "Shall I beat the bush, and another take the bird?" words which cost him the alliance of Burgundy, but added to the stock of English proverbs. Take, again, the history of "A burnt child dreads the fire." Starting simply from the "Even a fool after suffering gets him knowledge" of Hesiod, it then assumes a figurative form in Sophocles' "The fisherman when stung will get wisdom" (ἁλιεὺς πληγεὶς νοῦν οἴσει), a reference, the Scholiast tells us, to the saying of a fisherman who, too impatiently exploring the contents of his net and getting his hand wounded with the prickles of a scorpion fish, sensibly added, " But now that I have got stung, I shall be wiser." From Greek the proverb passed into Latin, " Piscator ictus sapit." In Italian it assumed another form, " Can scottato da l'acqua calda ha paura poi della fredda " (" A dog burnt by hot water, afterwards fears cold "). French follows with " Chien échaudé craint l'eau froide." In Spanish the dog becomes a cat ; it takes the form, " Gáto escaldado del agua ha miedo " ; and then comes the English form.

Thus most proverbs may be traced to the ancients, and it may be doubted whether in every hundred of them bearing on human character, on the virtues and vices, and on the conduct of life, there would be more than half a dozen which have not their precedents and archetypes in classical literature. So far back, indeed, stretches the pedigree of many of these proverbs that they were already proverbs when they were first cited. Thus Quintus Curtius tells us (Hist. vii. 4) that " His bark is worse than his bite " and " Still waters run deep " were proverbs among the Bactrians ; Quintilian tells us that " Liars should have good memories " was a proverb in his time, " Verum est illud quod vulgo dicitur, mendacem memorem esse oportere " (*Inst.* iv. 2, 91). " He is a wise child that knows his own father " is a deduction from a passage in the *Odyssey* (i. 216–7), where Telemachus says " My mother indeed says that I am his (child) ; for myself I know not, for

never man yet knew his own father." " A rolling
stone gathers no moss " is simply the translation
of a Greek verse, λίθος κυλινδομένος τὸ φῦκος οὐ ποιεῖ
—" moss " being substituted for " seaweed." To
Aristotle, in his turn quoting a proverb, we owe
" One swallow does not make spring " ; while
" As like as nail to nail " is a misapplied adaptation of another proverb quoted in his *Politics*
(viii. 12, 13), ἥλῳ γὰρ ὁ ἧλος, ὥσπερ ἡ παροιμία.
" Familiarity breeds contempt " is taken literally
from the Latin version of a sentence in Plutarch's
Morals, " Nimia familiaritas contemptum parit."
The well-known " De mortuis nihil nisi bonum "
is derived from Plutarch's " Life of Solon,"
where, speaking of Solon as a legislator, he says,
" That law is also justly commended which forbids men to speak ill of the dead : for piety re-
quires us to consider the dead as sacred," or
perhaps immediately from the saying of Chilo,
preserved by Diogenes Laertius, τὸν τεθνηκότα
μὴ κακολόγει (" Do not speak evil of the dead").
" The receiver is as bad as the thief " is a translation of a hexameter verse of Phocylides (ἀμφότεροι
κλῶπες, καὶ ὁ δεξάμενος καὶ ὁ κλέψας). " Bcttcr late
than never " we owe to Dionysius of Halicar-
nassus (ix. 11) : " It is better to begin late doing
our duties, than never." What is " Tread upon
a worm and it will turn " but the Greek ἔνεστι κἂν
μύρμηκι κἂν σέρφῳ χολή (" Even the ant, even
the gnat has its wrath "), and the Latin " Habet
et musca splenem," or " Set a thief to catch a
thief," but another turn of Cato's saw, " Ars
deluditur arte," or " An old bird is not caught

with chaff" but "Annosa vulpes haud capitur
laqueo" ("An old fox is not caught with a
snare"), or "The wrong end of the stick"
but the Greek "The hot end of the spit"
(τὸ θερμὸν τοῦ ὀβελοῦ)—a proverb preserved by
Sophocles—or "Two heads are better than one"
but an inferior version of the Greek εἷς ἀνὴρ οὐδεὶς
ἀνήρ ("One man no man")? So, "Coals to
Newcastle" is the exact equivalent of "Owls to
Athens," "Box to Cytorus," and the like.
The Greek proverb λαγὼς καθεύδων ("A hare
asleep"), which Pliny explains as meaning that
hares when asleep sleep with their eyes open,
finds an exact analogy in our "You won't catch
a weasel asleep," just as "Teaching one's grand-
mother," &c., is merely another form of the
Greek "Teaching an eagle to fly" or "dolphins
to swim." Again, "Out of the frying-pan into
the fire" and "Where there is smoke there is
fire" have their counterparts in εἰς τὸ πῦρ ἐκ
τοῦ κάπνου ("Into the fire out of the smoke")
and Plautus's "Flamma fumo est proxima"
("Flame is very close to smoke"). "God helps
those who help themselves" is simply a translation of the Latin proverb "Dii facientes adju-
vant," in its turn from the Greek σὺν Ἀθηνᾷ καὶ
χεῖρα κίνει ("With Minerva on your side, yet
use your own hand"), which reminds us, by the
way, of Cromwell's famous advice at the Battle
of Dunbar, "Trust in God and keep your powder
dry."

When we speak of "A tempest in a teapot"
we are only giving a modern application to a

phrase of Cicero, who, commenting on an attempt by one Gratidius to introduce the ballot at Arpinum, speaks of raising a storm in a saucer ("Fluctus excitare in simpulo"). When we speak of "Well done is half done," "Harping on the same string," "What cannot be cured must be endured," "Faults are soon copied," "Enough is as good as a feast," "Much would have more," "Much coin, much care," "A murrain take the hindmost," we are drawing on Horace. To Cicero we are indebted for "While there is life there is hope," though he quotes it as a proverb ("Aegroto dum anima, spes esse dicitur"); "Of two evils choose the least" (adapted, however, from Aristotle); while in his "Clitellae bovi sunt impositae" ("Panniers have been placed on an ox") and his "Duos parietes de eâdem fideliâ dealbare" ("To whitewash two walls from the same pot") we have analogues to our "Saddling the wrong horse" and "Killing two birds with one stone." In Lucian's ἡ ἅμαξα τὸν βοῦν ἕλκει ("The waggon drags the ox") we have the counterpart of our "Putting the cart before the horse"; and to the Greek Voltaire, as he has been well called, we are also indebted for the phrase "The dog in the manger" and its application. Among the many proverbs which may be traced to Plautus are "Getting blood out of a stone" ("Aquam a pumice postulare"), "What's done cannot be undone" ("Factum est illud; fieri infectum non potest"), "To throw cold water" on a thing ("Aquam frigidam subdole confundunt"), "A friend in need is a friend indeed" ("Is est amicus qui in dubiâ rejuvat, ubi re est opus"), "No flying without wings" ("Sine pennis volare haud facile est"), "Two heads are better than one" ("Nemo solus satis sapit"). "Virtue is its own reward," though a sentiment repeated in innumerable forms by the ancient philosophers, finds direct expression in the one really fine passage in Silius Italicus. Young Scipio is represented in the thirteenth book of the *Punica* as descending to Hades to visit the shades of his father and uncle, and on informing the shade of his father of the honours which had been done him on earth, the shade replies, "Virtue is, in itself, its own glorious reward" ("Ipsa quidem virtus sibimet pulcherrima merces"); but yet, he goes on to say, it is pleasing to the dead to know that the services they have done the living are not forgotten on earth (*Punica*, xiii. 663–66). "Better be envied than pitied" is a literal translation of the words of Herodotus, φθονέεσθαι κρέσσον ἔστιν ἢ οἰκτείρεσθαι. "Birds of a feather flock together" is simply a jingling adaptation of Homer's "God brings ever like to like," just as "Two of a trade can never agree" is deduced directly from Hesiod. To Menander we owe four famous proverbs: "Whom the Gods love die young," "Evil communications destroy good manners" (quoted by St. Paul), "When the tree has fallen, all go with their hatchet," and (though this reaches us immediately through Shakespeare) "Conscience makes cowards of us all."

To some classical proverbs which have become

naturalised in English a curious history is attached. Few probably know the history of " There's many a slip 'twixt the cup and the lip," which is a translation of the Greek proverb πολλὰ μεταξὺ πέλει κύλικος καὶ χείλεος ἄκρου. Ancæus, an ancient king of Samos, was fond of gardening, and planted some vines but was told by a prophet that he would never taste wine from them. Time went on, and the wine being duly made, Ancæus was lifting a cup of it to his lips, at the same time asking the prophet mockingly where his prophecy was now. " There are many things between the cup and the lip," replied the prophet. As he spoke, a loud tumult was heard outside, and Ancæus was told that a wild boar had broken in. Hurriedly putting the cup down without drinking, he rushed out to join the hunt against the boar, and was killed. And the prophet's remark, turned into a hexameter verse, passed into a proverb. The analogy to our " Bull in a china shop " is less tragical. A certain potter kept birds in his shop, and one day an ass, which his master was driving along, thrust his head into the shop and so frightened the birds that they in their wild flurry made havoc of the crockery. Upon that the potter sued the driver of the ass for damages ; but when he was asked to state the precise charge he had to bring, for neither the ass nor his master had directly done the damage, he replied, " On an ass's peeping in," hence the proverb. " Charity begins at home " we find in Theocritus, where it takes the form of " The shin is further than the knee " (ἀπωτέρω ἢ γόνυ

κνάμα) ; and in Plautus we find it in the form of
" The doublet is nearer than the cloak " (" Tunica
pallio proprior "), and more directly in Terence,
" I myself am nearest to myself" (" Proximus
sum egomet mihi "). But no proverb has a
pedigree more curious than the familiar " Conspicuous by his absence." This was first used by
Lord John Russell at a speech delivered at the
Guildhall on April 6, 1859, and was ridiculed in
the *Times*, or some other leading newspaper of
those times, as a bull. Upon that Lord John
defended it, and said it had been suggested to him
by a passage in Tacitus. Describing the funeral
of Junia, the wife of Caius Cassius, Tacitus says :
" The images of twenty of the most illustrious
families . . . were carried before it. Those of
Brutus and Cassius shone with a lustre the more
conspicuous from the simple reason that they
were not displayed " (*Annals*, iii. 76). Even the
famous " No man is a hero to his valet " may be
traced to a classical source ; for, though generally
attributed to either Madame de Sévigné or
to Madame Cornuël, it really belongs to Montaigne. " Peu d'hommes," he writes in the second
essay of his third book, " ont esté admirez par
leurs domestiques " ; and Montaigne got it, perhaps, from his favourite, Plutarch. In the essay
on Isis and Osiris, Plutarch archly observes,
speaking of certain glories attributed to a certain
person, " But his *valet de chambre* (λασαναφόρος)
told me he knew nothing of these things." We
should hardly have expected to find the proverb,
"The day after the fair," in Plato, and yet

it occurs in the " Gorgias," κατόπιν τῆς ἑορτῆς ἥκεις (" You have come after the feast "). To Publius Syrus we owe two proverbs which have a very modern ring about them, " A pleasant companion is as good as a coach " (" Comes facundus in viâ pro vehiculo est," *jucundus* being substituted) and " The smallest hair casts a shadow " (" Etiam capillus unus habet umbram suam ").

But we must not linger longer among the classics. Whoever would understand the nature and extent of the indebtedness of our proverbial literature to them should turn to the " Adagia " of Erasmus and the fragments of the Greek comic poets, where he will find an abundant harvest ungarnered even by the stupendous erudition of that scholar.

Another fertile source of current proverbs is to be found in the Fathers. We should hardly have expected to find in these grave and staid pundits such saws as " Love me, love my dog," and yet this has been preserved by St. Bernard, who quotes it as a proverb, " Qui me amat, amet et canem meum " ; or " We are in the same boat," which is a literal translation of a line in St. Clement's Epistle to the Church of Corinth (ἐν γὰρ τῷ αὐτῷ ἔσμεν σκάμματι) ; or,

He who will not, when he may,
When he will he shall have nay,

which originated thus. St. Basil was asked to plead the cause of a certain woman before the governor of a town, who replied that he would have helped her if he could ; but he could not, as the woman was a debtor to the treasury. Whereupon the Saint wrote in answer: "As you had the will to help her and could not, no harm was done; but had you been able to help her and would not, then Christ would have taken care that some day you should have the will without the power;" hence the proverb.

To St. Jerome we owe "One must not look a gift-horse in the teeth," though he quotes it as a proverb. The well-known "To do at Rome as the Romans do" has also a curious history. St. Augustine, for the satisfaction of his mother, Monica, asked St. Ambrose whether, as people in Rome fasted on Saturday, she should fast also on that day, though she was not accustomed to do so when at home. St. Ambrose replied, "When I am at home I do not fast on Saturday, but when I am at Rome I do; and I think you should follow the custom of every city you visit, if you would avoid scandal." From this originated a hexameter verse: "Cum Romae fueris, Romano vivite more" ("When you shall be at Rome, live after the Roman fashion"); hence the proverb. "An ounce of discretion is worth a pound of wit" is an adaptation of St. Gregory Nazianzen, "I prefer a drop of fortune to a casket of wit" (θέλω τυχῆς σταλαγμὸν ἢ φρενῶν πίθον), through a French proverb which is a literal translation of St. Gregory's words. The famous "Credo quia impossibile" ("I believe because it is impossible") is a truly extraordinary misapplication of a passage in Tertullian. Tertullian is commenting on Marcion's cavils at Christ's humanity: "The Son of God died, a fact quite credible because it is absurd; and after His burial He rose again, a fact quite certain because it is impossible."

Proverbs sometimes take their rise from simple facts. Thus, "Pouring oil on troubled waters" is derived from a fact known as early as the elder Pliny, who says, "All seas are made calm and still with oil" (*Nat. Hist.* ii. 103). So, "Patience is a flower that grows not in every one's garden," "Patience" being the vulgar name for a plant (the *Rhabarbarum monachorum* of botanists).

It is curious to note how many proverbs have either been deduced from misinterpretation or applications of texts from Scripture. A mere typographical blunder in our Authorised Version has given us the common saying, "Strain *at* a gnat and swallow a camel"—the more remarkable because all preceding versions, from Wiclif downward, had it right: "Strain *out* a gnat," the metaphor being, of course, taken from a strainer.

Another blunder in our Authorised Version, Psalm cxxvii. 2: "He giveth His beloved sleep," for "in sleep," has totally perverted the sense and given us a beautiful sentiment, of which there is no hint in the original. "Marriages are made in Heaven" is a deduction from Proverbs xix. 14, which first found expression in the French, "Les mariages se font en ciel," and then in more than one form in German, and appeared first in our language in 1639, when it is found in Clerk's "Paroemiologia." To a writer not known even by name to one reader in ten thousand we owe

the famous " Spare the rod and spoil the child "—
a variant, of course, of Proverbs xiii. 24: " He
that spareth his rod hateth his son." It first
appears in Davies of Hereford's " Scourge of
Folly," epigram 212, published in 1611: " To
spare the Rodd's to spill the child." Then it
appears in Thomas Draxe's " Bibliotheca Scholas-
tica," the preface of which is dated 1615, though
the work was not published till 1633; but it
owed its vogue, no doubt, to its insertion in
Clerk's " Paroemiologia " (1639) and Ray's " Proverbs." " Nothing succeeds like success " (" Rien
ne réussit comme le succès ") is simply a deduction
from St. Matthew xiii. 12: " To him that hath,
to him shall be given "; just as " Charity begins
at home," though anticipated by the Greeks, is
directly deduced from 1 Tim. v. 4: " Let them
learn to show piety at home and to requite their
parents." Some proverbs have sprung from
the most ludicrous perversions. For example,
" As sure as eggs is eggs " is a corruption of the
logician's announcement of identity, " X is X."
" Raining cats and dogs " is said to be a corruption of κατὰ δόξαν or δόξας (" as one might
expect "); but this is very doubtful. " Mad as a
hatter " (" Mad as a Natter "—an " adder "); to
" Know a hawk from a handsaw," where " handsaw " has been absurdly substituted for " hern-
shaw "—i.e. a heron. So " Sleeping like a top "
is said to have arisen from a misunderstanding
and mispronunciation of talpa, a mole—" Sleeping like a mole "; but this is not likely, as the
corresponding French proverb shows.

In some cases, as words and usages have become obsolete, proverbs have assumed a different form. A striking illustration of this is found in the well-known phrase, "Setting the Thames on fire," which most probably originated from a confusion between "Thames" and *temse* (a sieve). In former times, before the days of machinery, flour was sent from the mill unsifted; it was then sifted by means of a "temse," a word not yet obsolete in Yorkshire and Lincolnshire. This "temse" was worked over the mouth of the barrel into which the meal was sifted, and when plied very vigorously became so hot, by force of friction against the metal rim of the flour-barrel, that it almost got on fire. Hence it was said of a languid or unskilful sifter that he would never "set the temse on fire." The transition to "Thames" and with a slightly different application of the proverb became easy and natural; but in this form the proverb has not, I believe, been traced beyond Foote. We have an analogy in "Don't lose the sheep (or ship) for a ha'porth o' tar," which had one meaning in the inland counties and another in maritime. In the former it referred to dabbing the wound of a sheep, which had lacerated itself, with tar; in the latter to caulking a ship or boat. Another curious double application of meaning we find in the phrase, "Putting a spoke in his wheel," which is direct from the Dutch, "Een spaak in 't wiel steeken," and means to cross or thwart a design or intention—in other words, to impede or lock the wheel; but it is now often used in the opposite

meaning of aiding or assisting, strengthening a
man's wheel. " Good wine needs no bush " takes
us back to the days when a bush was a sign over
tavern doors, a custom traditionally derived
from the ancient Roman custom of hanging out
a branch of ivy, the emblem of Bacchus, over
their *tabernæ ;* just as the phrase " By hook or
by crook " takes us back to the times of the im-
memorial " right of firewood," when the hook
was used for cutting the green wood and the
crook for breaking off the dry and raking together
what had been cut down. An accomplishment
for which we were once pre-eminent among
European nations has left a deep impress on our
proverbial literature, such as " Always have two
strings to your bow," " A fool's bolt is soon
shot," " Draw not the bow before the arrow be
fixed," " It is no sure rule to fish with a cross-
bow," " Heaven save the mark ! " said ironically
when an unskilful archer was about to shoot, and
the like. In " Give an inch and he'll take an ell "
we are in the world of the Jewish usurers who
were the pest of mediæval Spain, the proverb
being directly from the Spanish, " Al Judio dá-lhe
un palmo, y tomará quadro." " Hobson's choice "
takes us back to the Cambridge of Milton's time,
when Tobias Hobson, the carrier between Cambridge and London, had so prospered in his business that he was able to set up some livery stables.
His rule was, that those who applied to him for
a hack were not allowed to make any selection
from those which stood for hire, but were
obliged to take the one which came first in order

in the stable, or, in the case of that being engaged, the second, and so in rotation ; and to this annoying regulation he would make no exception, so that Hobson's choice became a proverb in the University for no choice at all. A well-known French proverb has a similarly curious local origin : " Pour un point Martin perdit son âne," applied to illustrate the importance of trifles. One Martino, the abbot of the abbey of Asello, ordered a Latin inscription—of questionable Latinity certainly—to be inscribed over the principal gate, " Porta placens esto nulli claudaris honesto "—that is, " Mayest thou never be closed, O friendly gate, to any honest person ! " but the stupid sculptor put a comma after " nulli," so that the meaning became " Be, O gate, kindly to no one; mayest thou be shut to an honest person." Unhappily the Pope happened to pass by, and, observing the inscription, deprived Martin of the abbey and gave it to another, who, receiving it unwillingly, as he was the friend of poor Martin, substituted " Pro solo puncto caruit Martinus Asello " (" For a comma alone was Martin deprived of Asello "), hence the proverb.

To a story preserved by Plutarch we owe the origin of the often-quoted " None knows where the shoe pinches but him who wears it." The passage is in his *Life of Æmilius Paullus*, and he tells the anecdote, not directly of Æmilius, as Disraeli wrongly represents, but in relation to his divorce from Papiria. " A certain Roman having forsaken his wife, her friends fell out with him, and asked him what fault he found in her ;

was she not faithful and fair, and had she not borne him many beautiful children ? " He replied by putting forth his foot and saying, " Is not this a goodly shoe ? Is it not finely made, and is it not new ? And yet I dare say there is not one of you who can tell me where it wrings me." To Plutarch we also owe the preservation of another very popular saying, " Talis cum sis utinam noster esses ! " (" Being such a one as you are, would that you were on our side ! ") This was said by Agesilaus to Pharnabazus, the Persian general ; but probably owed its currency as a proverb to Bacon, who, referring to their enthusiasm in education and learning, applies it to the Jesuits. Many popular proverbs owe their origin to the shrewdness and wit of obscure people, and their vogue to their preservation or adoption by famous men. Such would be " What is every man's business is nobody's business," which did not originate, as is commonly supposed, from Lord Chesterfield, but from " a wise friend " of Izaak Walton's. " I remember that a wise friend of mine did usually say, ' That which is everybody's business is nobody's business ' " (" Complete Angler, part i. chap. 2) ; while Lord Chesterfield has, by recording, helped to immortality a casual remark made by a certain Mr. Lowndes, a Secretary of the Treasury in William III.'s time, to one of the officials under him : " Take care of the pence, and the pounds will take care of themselves."

More than one famous proverb has been boldly extemporised, and then assigned to some well-known but voluminous writer, and so passed

s

muster for generations. Such is the famous " Les Anglais s'amusent tristement " (" The English take their pleasures sadly "), so confidently ascribed to Froissart but not to be found in either him or in any French author. To the same category belongs " Suaviter in modo, fortiter in re," assigned sometimes to Cicero and sometimes to Pliny but to be found in no Roman author at all. It has been concocted by some one either from the Latin Vulgate (*Wisdom of Solomon*, viii. 1), " Attingit ergo a fine ad finem fortiter, et disponit omnia suaviter," or from a writer of the early seventeenth century, Claudius Aquaviva (*Ad Curandos Animæ Morbos*, cap. ii.): " It will easily be seen how we should be firm in the pursuit of our end and gentle in our mode of pursuing " (" Fortes in fine consequendo et suaves in modo assequendi "). The saying " Go to Jericho ! " has probably passed through the same process. Jericho, which was a house in the Manor of Blackmore, about seven miles from Chelmsford, was, so Haywarde tells us, one of Henry VIII.'s " houses of pleasure," and when he was " desirous of not being disturbed, the answer given was that he had gone to Jericho ; in other words, that he was not at home." His Majesty's recreations at Jericho do not appear to have been very reputable, and the phrase " Gone to Jericho," or " Go to Jericho," passed with his facetious courtiers into a proverb implying more than met the ear. A generation or two afterwards it no doubt either became confounded with the Biblical Jericho or at all events lost its original significance, and became a synonym with retirement or banishment. To another of our kings we owe, so it has been asserted, a far more famous proverb, " Those who live in glass houses shouldn't throw stones." It seems that Villiers, afterwards first Duke of Buckingham, took great exception to the Scotchmen who came pouring into England in the wake of our first Scotch king, and, putting himself at the head of certain riotous youths, stoned the windows of some of them. In retaliation they broke the windows of his house, which was known as the Glasshouse, in St. Martin's fields. Upon that Villiers complained to the king, who punningly replied, " Ah ! Steenie, those who live in glass houses shouldn't throw stones." This certainly savours of the apocryphal, and Professor Skeat attempts to explode it by pointing out that the proverb is as old as Chaucer's time, quoting "Troilus and Criseyde," ii. 867 ; but the passage is not at all parallel. Chaucer merely says that a man whose head is made of glass had better keep it out of reach of the stones of a battlefield. So far as I can discover, the proverb is not to be found till after the time of James I. ; it appears, I believe, for the first time in Herbert's " Jacula Prudentum," published in 1640, in this form : " Whose house is of glass, must not throw stones at another." James's facility in coining aphorisms is well known, and the story may be true. To a very pathetic incident we owe the famous " Experimentum in corpore vili." The celebrated scholar Muretus was taken ill at a town in Lombardy, and two physicians were called in to attend him. Seeing that he was a poor man, and not knowing who he was, they determined to try an experiment on him, one saying to the other in Latin, a language of which they supposed he was ignorant, " Faciamus experimentum in animâ vili " (" Let us try the experiment on a life which is of no account ") ; but from the patient came the words, " Vilem animam appellas pro quâ Christus non dedignatus est mori ? " (" Callest thou that a life of no account for which Christ did not disdain to die ? ") So with the alteration of " animâ " to " corpore " came the phrase which has since been current.

Nothing is so difficult in many cases as to trace proverbs to their sources—to determine whether when they first appear they are quoted or coined. This is particularly the case with Chaucer, with Shakespeare, with the Elizabethan dramatists, and with Swift, among our own writers, and with Dante, Cervantes and Rabelais on the Continent. Chaucer, for example, had long the credit of the happy expression " To make a virtue of necessity," but it has been traced to sources long antecedent to him, the earliest being Matthew Paris, " Faciendo de necessitate virtutem." Marlowe has been credited with " Love me little, love me long," introduced into " The Rich Jew of Malta," but it has been traced to an anonymous ballad printed in 1569, and probably goes back to a date still earlier.

Of the innumerable proverbs in Shakespeare it is impossible to determine which he coined and which he quoted—whether, for instance

" A light heart lives long," " A knavish speech
sleeps in a foolish ear," " Brevity is the soul of
wit," " He that dies pays all debts," and the like
were his own coinage. So with Swift, to whom,
however, undoubtedly belongs the ninth beatitude, " Blessed is he that expecteth nothing."

How difficult it is to be sure of the real source
of a proverb is strikingly illustrated by the
famous phrase " The greatest happiness of the
greatest number," which got its currency from
Bentham. Bentham himself said that he owed it
either to Priestley or to Beccaria, and it is found
in Beccaria's introduction to his " Essay on
Crimes and Punishments," where it assumes the
form of " La massima felicità divisa nel maggior
numero " ; but nearly forty years before Beccaria's work appeared the very phrase had occurred
in English in Hutcheson's " Inquiry into the
Origin of our Ideas of Beauty and Virtue " :
" That action is best which accomplishes *the
greatest happiness for the greatest number.*" A
very curious history is attached to the famous
" Ridicule is the test of truth," so long attributed
to Shaftesbury. The Shaftesburian authorship
was exploded by Carlyle, who after a careful search
was unable to find it anywhere in Shaftesbury's
writings ; adding that " of all chimæras that
ever advanced themselves in the shape of philosophical doctrines, this is to us the most inconceivable." Since then the proverb has gone
fatherless. But it belongs, if I am not mistaken,
to Akenside the poet, who has, in the notes to the
third book of " The Pleasures of the Imagina-

tion," advanced it, not as a quotation from
Shaftesbury but as a deduction of his own from
Shaftesbury philosophy which he is combating.
The passage runs: "To ask them whether
ridicule be a test of truth is, in other words, to
ask whether that which is ridiculous can be
morally true, can be just and becoming, or
whether that which is just and becoming can be
ridiculous." Thus by substituting the definite
for the indefinite article an aphorism has been
coined expressing seriously as a truth what its
originator designed as the *reductio ad absurdum*
of a fallacy which he was refuting. When Dr.
Johnson sadly observed, "Sir, Hell is paved
with good intentions," he may be said to have
reminted in gold what before existed only in the
poor copper of Herbert's "Hell is full of good
meanings and wishings," and the Spanish "El
infierno es lleno de buenas intenciones." On one
occasion Dr. Johnson did rap out a saying which
has become a proverb, attributing it to "an
ancient writer." In one of his visits to Oxford
he met a certain Mr. Mortimer, who was continually interrupting him with contradiction:
"Sir, I deny that," and again, "I utterly deny
it." At last Johnson, irritated almost to madness,
roared out, "Sir, if you deny that, I can only say,
with an ancient writer, 'Plus in unâ horâ negabit
unus asinus quam centum philosophi in centum
annis probaverint' ('A single ass will deny more
in a single hour than a hundred philosophers
have made good in a hundred years')." To Lord
Mansfield is attributed "The greater the truth

the greater the libel," though it is, of course, a simple deduction from the law. From the language of the law, by the way, have been deduced many popular proverbs, such as " Forewarned is forearmed " (" Præmoniti, præmuniti "), " Necessity knows no law " (" Necessitas non habet legem "), " Illgotten gains never prosper " (" Male parta male dilabuntur "), " A man's house is his castle," deduced from " Jura publica favent privato domûs " (" The law favours the privacy of a home "); while in " Nullum medicamentum est idem omnibus " (" No remedy is the same for all ") we have perhaps the original of " What is one man's meat is another man's poison."

If the political history of a nation may be read in its ballads, nowhere are its moral, intellectual and social characteristics written so legibly as in its proverbs, in those which it has originated, which it has borrowed, which it has recoined and in various ways modified.

INDEX

THE BALLANTYNE PRESS TAVISTOCK STREET COVENT GARDEN LONDON

Redwood Library

SELECTIONS FROM THE RULES

1. Three volumes may be taken at a time and only three on one share. Two unbound numbers of a monthly and three numbers of a weekly publication are counted as a volume.

2. Books other than 7-day and 14-day ones may be kept out 28 days. *Books cannot be renewed or transferred.*

3. Books overdue are subject to a fine of one cent a day for fourteen days, *and five cents a day for each day thereafter.*

4. Neglect to pay the fine will debar from the use of the Library.

5. No book is to be lent out of the house of the person to whom it is charged.

6. Any person who shall soil (deface) or damage or lose a book belonging to the Library shall be liable to such fine as the Directors may impose; or shall pay the value of the book or of the set, if it be a part of a set, as the Directors may elect. All scribbling or any marking or writing whatever, folding or turning down the leaves, as well as cutting or tearing any matter from a book belonging to the Library, will be considered defacement and damage.